THE FAITHS OF IRELAND

Stephen Skuce

The Faiths of Ireland

the columba press

First published in 2006 by
the columba press
55A Spruce Avenue, Stillorgan Industrial Park,
Blackrock, Co Dublin

Cover by Bill Bolger
Origination by The Columba Press
Printed in Ireland by ColourBooks Ltd, Dublin

ISBN 1 85607 525 7

Table of Contents

Acknowledgements

Like all authors I have many people to thank for helping me write this book.

Revd Dudley Cooney has been a generous, supportive critic of my work. Revd Dr Norman Taggart has provided scholarly advice and encouragement. Revd Dr Dennis Cooke has expertly guided my research, some of which has developed into this text and I have been assisted latterly, in a similar way, by Revd Dr Richard Clutterbuck. Portions of this book have been generously read by Irish people who are members of some of the religious traditions considered here and they include Edwin Graham, Darragh Monahan and Heather Abrahamson. I am more than grateful to the colleagues with whom I have shared with, in a small way, in the work of the Institute of Theology at Queens University, Belfast, The Irish Bible Institute, St Patrick's College, Drumcondra and the University College Dublin Chaplaincy team.

There have been too many to mention who have encouraged me with my interest in this aspect of Irishness. Any wisdom in this book is a result of their conversations and challenges while the errors remain my own.

Finally I owe the most to Marlene, Amy and Bethany who give me happiness beyond my dreams.

Introduction

Ireland has changed, is changing and always will be changing. The question 'What does it mean to be Irish?' is never static but reflects a dynamic environment. Part of what this book seeks to achieve is to show that Ireland's contemporary religious landscape is a new experience; the census returns alone show this clearly, but it is not a unique experience. A brief look into Ireland's past will recover knowledge of the story of interreligious encounters. The histories of the various faith communities settled in Ireland point to substantial Irish contact with many different religious communities for over a thousand years. Ireland has experienced various religious changes and current developments are simply part of that process.

Census returns are only bare statistics, colourless. Ireland, past and present, is replete with fascinating and intriguing interfaith encounters. I hope this work will make some of these stories better known so that they can be acknowledged as Irish history, as much as any other event that has taken place on this island or has been affected by Irish people.

As is consistent with Irish history, the story is not all positive. One of my surprises when researching this book was to realise that in the recent Irish conflict victims have included Muslims, Hindus, Sikhs and Jews. I rechecked my sources for my initial reaction was that these faith communities must be far too small to have been caught up in a local sectarian campaign. Yet the sad truth is there. In a conflict caricatured as a Protestant-Catholic dispute the old Ulster joke of whether someone is a Protestant Jew or a Catholic Jew sounds very hollow when the list of victims is read. Perhaps this points us to greater non-Christian faith involvement in Ireland than many had previously realised. These small faith communities have suffered alongside the rest of us from the majority Christian community. They have paid a heavy price to belong here. Those of us from what might loosely be called the 'host community' need to rediscover our past to better understand our present and hopefully move to a better future.

Chapter One briefly considers Ireland's history from an inter-religious perspective. Chapter Two recounts the historic inter-faith experience of Irish women and men as they have travelled throughout the world. Chapters Three to Seven detail the hist-ories of various faith communities in Ireland, how each commu-nity has adapted to Ireland and contributed to making Ireland what it is today. A significant part of these chapters considers the beliefs and practices of the various faiths surveyed. While there is no shortage of description of religious faiths, here the consistent approach is to consider the beliefs and practices of Irish Muslims, Irish Jews and so on. Chapter Eight uncovers Ireland's national history of interreligious understanding, co-operation, avoidance and dialogue. Finally, Chapter Nine is a personal reflection, based on what has gone before, as to how Ireland's developing context offers us a future better than our present and so much better than our past.

It is my hope that this work will be of interest to all who have a stake in Ireland, to those who work among Ireland's newer cit-izens, to participants in world history, to the Irish diaspora who may discover they are living among friends not strangers, to third level students studying the general area of religion in Ireland and the specific area of world religions, and to those who are interested enough to want to know more about their neighbour.

This book reflects the pluralism of contemporary and future Ireland. Pluralism, as the presence of various religious perspec-tives, is a fact of life in Ireland. What this book does not do is promote pluralism as an ideology that considers all views as ei-ther equally valid or equally irrelevant. That is not my personal viewpoint. I feel passionately that Ireland must be an accepting, open and plural society. Yet that does not mean that those of us who are Christian by background, upbringing and conviction simply see ourselves as travelling along one road among many.

This book will lay out the reality of Ireland's non-Christian faith communities and their beliefs today. Other works and scholars need to reflect more on how we understand each other. If this book is a small stimulus in that process it will have been worthwhile.

CHAPTER ONE

The Historic Irish Inter-Faith Experience

Ireland has been a mixture of cultures for millennia. What is exported throughout the world as 'Irish culture', be it a theme bar or *Riverdance*, is a combination of disparate elements brought together. This is how it has always been. The pure Irish culture, however that may be defined, is a very elusive creature. If today Ireland is being seen as an emerging melting pot of Irish, British, western and increasing eastern European cultures, with a flavouring of African and Asian, what is new is that Ireland is being seen this way. We have always been a composite people.

At times various differing worldviews have coexisted in Ireland, not always peacefully. In 1895 two of Dublin's more sophisticated individuals were engaged in legal combat in London that held the chattering classes of the British Isles spellbound. While Edward Carson was cross-examining Oscar Wilde in the infamous libel case, in rural Tipperary Bridget Cleary was burnt to death by her husband. After a trial that was almost as sensational for Ireland, Bridget's husband Michael Cleary, a farm labourer, was sentenced to ten years for manslaughter. Rather than this being a brutal act of jealousy or rage, Cleary argued that he was actually trying to save his wife's life rather than kill her. He was under the impression that fairies had taken his wife and replaced her with a weak 'changeling', hence the illness from which she was suffering.

Was Cleary exhibiting paranoid delusion? Apparently not, according to the court, the doctors, the prison system and the local population. Cleary had been assisted by a number of relatives and friends over a period of several days as he attempted to drive away the fairy changeling and regain his wife. Living near a supposed fairy fort at Kylenagranagh, Co Tipperary, Cleary and others became convinced that Bridget's illness was due to her being taken by fairies and replaced by a changeling. The only way to deal with this was to drive the fairy out by fire. After this had been done, Cleary would wait at midnight near the fairy fort when his true wife would ride by on a white horse. If he could cut the cords that tied his wife to the steed then she would be freed, otherwise she would be lost forever.

The incident did not have a happy ending. After holding his wife over a fire for just a few moments one evening, the following night Cleary and his wife's cousins made a second attempt with disastrous consequences. Bridget's nightdress caught fire and Cleary appeared to dowse her with oil from a nearby lamp. Soon his wife was totally engulfed in flames and died, presumably in extreme agony. Cleary buried the body and waited by the fairy fort for his true wife to ride by. It was, of course, only the police who appeared in order to arrest him.

This incident illustrates an enduring acceptance of pre-Christian beliefs within a rural Irish community at the dawn of the twentieth century. A religious framework that may have seemed to have been replaced by Christianity fifteen hundred years previously clearly still existed. In a late nineteenth century world of trains, newspapers and rapid advancement, a belief in fairies still dramatically impacted a rural Irish community. Bizarre though much of this may sound to some of us, the phrases 'he is not himself' and 'she's away with the fairies' are still in common speech. Perhaps primal Irish religious understanding still has a hold on us. So what was the earliest Irish religious understanding?

About 6000 years before the Celtic Tiger made Ireland a 'must see' destination, farmers, probably from Spain or Portugal, pushed their small currach-style craft holding their family and a couple of cows or sheep into the ocean and headed for Ireland. Settling in the Boyne valley they found food, extensive forests and a plentiful supply of drinking water. To immortalise their prosperity they wanted a temple to thank the gods. Built over

1000 years before the Egyptian pyramids, today we call that place Newgrange.

The exact purpose of Newgrange, arguably one of the most impressive megalithic sites in Europe, is still a mystery but religion had to be a very strong element in this collection of burial chambers. Built around 3000BC and considered to be a Temple to Dagda, the sun god, it is built so that the sun's rays penetrate into the centre of the cruciform chamber inside the circular cairn during the winter solstice, 21 December. Other prehistoric sites such as Stonehenge in England are orientated around midsummer's day, 21 June, when the sun is at its strongest. It appears the primary purpose was as a burial chamber, as indicated by the presence of cremated human remains, although it may have been reserved as a royal burial site rather than as a community site as the amount of these remains is relatively small. The religious beliefs that can be discerned from Newgrange seem to be related to the seasons, with the sun possibly worshipped as a god. The burial chambers point to some sort of belief in an afterlife, the absence of tools or weapons possibly suggesting a future life devoid of the need for work or fighting. It could be that Newgrange's alignment to 'capture' the sun's rays at their weakest helped to create a link between death and new life, with the rays growing stronger from 21 December onwards. Standing stones around the edge of the mound seem to signify a lunar involvement in the religious practices. Whether this can be equated with religion in a formalised sense is debatable but Newgrange still justifies a 'religious' label as an expression of the beliefs of the community.

We do not know for certain what happened to these people. Possibly a new influx of immigrants we have come to call the Celts drove them out around 400BC or a new community peacefully intermingled with the original, or new ideas coming through peaceful trading contacts simply helped the Newgrange Irish to develop. It is impossible to say. Yet a change did occur and the Celtic people, sharing a common ethnic identity through much of central and western Europe, put their religious mark on

Ireland in a possibly more permanent way than the community of Newgrange.

With the exception of the northern extremities of Scotland, Ireland was the only Celtic area not to be conquered by Rome, although recent discoveries do point to a few limited and temporary Roman settlements in the greater Dublin area. Roman coins, pottery and broaches have been found in a few locations that generally were thought to be the remnants of Roman traders but current scholarship points to possibly a more permanent, if limited, residence. In the first four centuries after the birth of Christ, Irish Celtic society was a complex arrangement of kings and nobles, with noblewomen prominent. Four provinces were in existence with a possible fifth province of Meath, and while High Kings existed, just how far their rule extended is hard to discern. While there is little evidence that points to a Celtic invasion of Ireland, there would have been trading links with Britain and France and small scale movements of people. Society comprised a complex arrangement of raths (small ring forts), crannogs (artificial islands) and more extensive hill forts, with the population living by cultivation of the land, rearing cows, sheep and pigs, and some hunting. Pottery and jewellery of gold and bronze were prominent, both showing links to the wider Celtic world, especially France, albeit with Irish distinction in decoration.

The religion of the Celts is hard to define, although the abandonment of Newgrange illustrates a distinct change in religious practice. A new way of belief had come. Knowledge of this Celtic belief comes almost exclusively from the Christian recording in word of the oral tradition of myths and legends, but a Christian bias in this recording cannot be discounted. The group of legends known as the Ulster Cycle containing the 'Cattle Raid of Cooley', describe an independent Celtic culture contemporary with the Roman world where honour, strength in battle and glory appeared to have more appeal than even life itself. These and similar tales portray gods who could deceive people by changing their shape and who were under the influence of the

Druids. They often ruled as kings (such as Dagda of the Tuatha Dé Danaan) but on the arrival of the Celts they retreated to live in mounds. People attempted to please these gods and feared to offend them. In addition to a pantheon of gods, the earth itself was significant as the 'mother' giving life, as were wells, springs and rivers that often had gods or goddesses associated with them.

Four seasonal religious festivals were celebrated, with the Druids perpetuating this system, conducting the ceremonies, teaching of an immortal soul passing from one body to another and practising divination. The Druids held a position in society akin to that of the Hindu Brahmins. Kings could not make decisions without their approval and while the Druids were not the rulers, their wishes were carried out. The burial of food with a body implies this afterlife was a real continuation, to be spent in a 'Land of the Young', possibly below or beyond the sea. In the inter-faith encounter, Celtic religion defeated the Newgrange understanding. Celtic belief was to be strongly challenged by the next faith to enter Ireland, but would continue in a partially hidden way, arguably up to the present day.

Whether it was through St Patrick, a number of Patricks, Palladius, various unknown evangelists or whoever, the primal religion of the existing Celtic population was soon Christianised in a relatively painless process around the fifth century when Roman power in Britain and elsewhere was starting to decline. Irish society, especially in the east, was experiencing greater trading links with Britain and Europe but her warlike nature still made Ireland a country to be feared. Trading links with countries as far away as the eastern Mediterranean potentially existed as early as 450AD. Egyptian glass fragments found in Co Cork appear to belong to this date. As a consequence, the inter-faith experience of Ireland includes interaction between Ireland and Egypt before Christianity triumphed in Ireland and before Islam had even been revealed.

The absence of martyrs alludes to the relative ease with which Christianity was adopted in Ireland, or alternatively to the relatively small changes that were required from the population to convert. For example the Celtic festival of Samhain was christianised into 'All Saints Day', but still retained its force as the season of Halloween. This ease of change may have been aided by the absence of systematic organisation in Celtic religion. While Celtic religion did have its rituals, festivals and priestly class in the druids and through the poets, its localised nature meant it was ill equipped to withstand a coherent, developed religious opposition. This experience was paralleled in nineteenth and early twentieth century African history, where Muslim and Christian evangelists were both able to make rapid inroads in areas of Traditional African Religion. In Ireland the Christian festivals and clergy were able to supplant their unorganised predecessors although it can be argued that early Christianity simply adopted Celtic religious practices with very little change.

Almost certainly Patrick found some Christians already present in Ireland, yet even if the Patrick legends are stripped away there is still a charismatic leader, evangelist and organiser. In Muirchú's seventh century *Life of St Patrick*, there is an account of a contest with druids where Patrick responded to their magic with a greater show of strength. When the druids make snow, only Patrick can make it vanish, when the druids put poison in his cup Patrick can make the drink freeze and the poison fall out. Eventually King Laoire is converted to Christianity through this demonstration of divine power, and so the first documented inter-faith experience in Ireland is recorded as the triumphant progress of a Christian missionary overcoming the indigenous religion, a pattern that would be repeated in much worldwide missionary writing. However, this record is probably far from accurate, being written long after the event to support the position of Armagh as the primal see of Ireland. The Roman ecclesiastical system of dioceses, based on provincial towns with a surrounding hinterland, did not fit into the non-urbanised Celtic lifestyle of Ireland where federations of monastic communities developed, each with their own *parochia* under the authority of the successor to the founder of the main monastery.

The survival of some Celtic practices within Christianity is of great significance in the inter-faith experience of Ireland. It alludes to a syncretistic understanding whereby the new religion was comfortable enough or perhaps confident enough to absorb some pre-existing customs and beliefs and to some extent merge them with Christianity. While this did not create a new religion out of Celtic faith and Christianity, the clear distinction of 'Celtic Christianity', still existing to some extent in the twenty first century, does demonstrate that Celtic religion has shaped Christianity in a similar way to that in which other primal religious beliefs have come to shape Christianity in some other cultures.

When the Celtic religion had overcome the Newgrange belief the great mound was abandoned as a place of worship, worshippers being replaced by grazing sheep. Within Celtic Christianity many of the early churches were built on the sites of Celtic religious places, saints were adaptations of Celtic mythical figures and Patrick himself is portrayed as a Celtic hero. If the first inter-faith encounter resulted in an abandoning of Newgrange faith, the second encounter arguably resulted in the underground triumph of Celtic religion rather than the overwhelming triumph of Christianity that is often portrayed.

In 795 the first sight of a Viking longboat off the Antrim coast must have been greeted with great interest, with the dimensions of these ocean-going crafts much superior to the small Irish boats. Interest rapidly turned to fear and so began the next Irish inter-faith encounter in the eighth to eleventh centuries. Just why the Vikings suddenly descended on western Europe from Norway, Sweden and Denmark is unclear, although an increasing population needing more land and goods may have been a factor. When this was combined with the technology to build ships capable of lengthy spells at sea and of carrying significant numbers, attacks on Ireland became inevitable. The Vikings combined a sophisticated technology with an aggressive approach to others, raiding rather than trading being their early interaction with Ireland. Monasteries and churches were among the first places of encounter between the Christian Irish and the pagan Viking, but rather than searching for inter-faith under-standing the Vikings came to steal the wealth of the community that was often stored in these settlements. There was a religious dimension to this encounter in that often clerics, seen as provid-ing leadership within communities, were singled out to be killed. The shrines were viewed as the focal point of the commu-nity and to destroy the community's ability to fight back, these focal points were ransacked. A further inter-faith dimension can be seen in the designation the Irish gave to these unwelcome visitors, that of *gentes* or 'pagans'. Initially the Vikings only raided the coastal regions and returned either to Scandinavia or to places where they had put down more permanent roots such as the Scottish islands, but over the years they began to winter and then to settle permanently in towns such as Dublin, Limerick and Waterford. Over time these Vikings were subsumed into the Irish population and the Christian faith was adopted. After his conversion to Christianity the Viking King Sitric of Dublin established Donatus as the first Bishop of Dublin at Christ Church, probably in 1038.

Knowledge of the Viking religion comes largely from Christian writings, many of which are Icelandic, and conse-quently this knowledge suffers from a possible bias, although we do have the Arab chronicler Ibn Fadlan's record of a pagan Viking funeral on the Volga. The use of ships in burials indicated that death was considered to be a journey with an afterlife of drinking and fighting in Valhalla being the destination. Different regions had different gods, Odin and Thor being sig-nificant, followed by a vast array of minor deities, often as part of family groups. These gods spent their time fighting other gods, giants and monsters, and influencing the course of events. Sacred groves, islands, meadows and rivers all featured with the necessary rituals carried out by priests.

The Viking era ended with the victory of Christianity over the Viking faith. As such this was the first time a new wave of immigrants had failed to gain religious ascendancy over the indigenous population in Ireland. The factors that led to this arguably included the relative lack of political control the Vikings exerted over Ireland as a whole, the looseness of their religious practices and the Viking tendency to merge with the existing population over time. However, it is still worth stressing that while the Celts overcame Newgrange religion and had many of their beliefs and practices incorporated into Christianity, the original Viking faith largely died out.

One factor is sometimes not given enough weight. Some of the Vikings who arrived in Ireland by the tenth century may well have arrived as Christians. Missionary efforts by monks such as Ansgar of Germany who travelled with the exiled King Harald Klak of Denmark between 826 and 829 had resulted in Viking Christian populations and the Danes formally became Christians around 960. In Sweden this process took longer but in Norway King Olaf Haraldsson, ruling from 1015-1031, was renowned for his vigorous defence of his new faith, gaining the title of St Olaf. Some of the later Vikings must have come to Ireland as Christians and so it is not that surprising that the Viking religion did not make a significant impact in Ireland for, at the same time, it was losing ground in Scandinavia. This process could have been helped by a relatively detached view of religion expressed by poets such as the Icelandic Eilif Gudrunarson who was able to write in praise of both Christ and Thor around the year 1000.

It is interesting to speculate on one further factor of the Viking involvement in Ireland. Through Viking trading and their slave trade Irish people almost certainly came into significant contact with Muslims, Hindus and Buddhists for the first time. The Vikings traded with the Baltic region and reached Islamic countries via the river Volga. Irish slaves were captured to be sold since the Vikings were the major slave-traders of their day, chiefly supplying the Islamic Empire. Excavations in Helgo, Sweden have uncovered treasure trove containing a bronze figure of the Buddha from northern India together with an Irish inlaid bronze mount that was possibly a crozierhead. Multi-faith Ireland was beginning. The emergence of the

Vikings started to expose Ireland, albeit in a limited way, to the religions of Asia whereas the earlier freedom from Roman control had helped to keep Ireland religiously immune from wider influences.

The arrival of the Normans in the eleventh century brought another wave of invaders that continued through the Middle Ages into the time of Cromwell and successive plantations into the seventeenth century. These are not of direct concern here as they were successive waves of nominally Christian invaders and settlers. The varieties within the experiences of Christianity in Ireland are sufficient for commentators to talk about the Protestant and Roman Catholic *religions* but the intra-Christian encounter should not be designated as an inter-faith event. Interaction between Christian communities should rather be viewed in the same way as, for example, the arrival of both Sunni and Shi'a Muslims in Ireland. The differences between the individual expressions of the one faith may be great, so great indeed that some devotees find it impossible to worship with each other or even to consider the other as authentically following the same faith. Be that as it may, fundamentally these are differences within a religion and not between religions.

What this consideration of the earliest Irish interreligious experiences illustrates is that religious change is not a new experience for Ireland. Of course, within the Irish Christian community there have been many cataclysmic moments of change due to conquest, plantation or independence. But the recent Irish experience of new religious communities settling and making an impact on the religious geography of the nation is far from unique. This has been the ongoing experience from earliest times and the relatively unchallenged supremacy of Christianity from the fourth to the nineteenth century is more the exception rather than the norm.

As we look at the interaction of more modern Irish people with people of other faiths abroad, and then at how followers of various world religions have come to Ireland, made their home here and adapted to life in Ireland, it is placed within this context of normality. This has been our experience. We are all descendants of waves of immigrants with distinctive religious understandings, whether we trace our roots back to the Celts, Normans, English, Scottish or whoever. Just who we might claim to be is really determined on what date in history we stop at. To go further back widens the gene pool rather than narrowing or purifying it. Perhaps those who claim a direct and undiluted Viking descent can stand aloof from this, as their primal religious understanding did not continue in Ireland. Can anyone claim such a 'pure' descent? It is extremely doubtful. Perhaps that understanding will help remind us that what we may perceive as distinct ethnic and religious differences, enough to make an 'us' and 'them', are nothing more than stages in a shared evolution. What does it mean to be Irish? Hopefully it is the choice to make your home on this island, with a resultant unity between the interconnected descendants of Celts and Vikings, Protestants and Catholics, Jews and Muslims and whoever else comes among us and becomes part of us.

CHAPTER TWO

The Irish Abroad

Until the twentieth century Irish people had relatively little contact with representatives of Hinduism, Buddhism and Islam within Ireland. But that was not the case abroad and, given the Irish ability to travel widely, it is not surprising that it was primarily abroad that the Irish started to interact with followers of the great world faiths.

How many Hindu gods come from Co Tyrone? Well, not many but there is at least one whose statue still adorns the entrance to his old school. General Sir John Nicholson was a ruthless Victorian British army officer, initially seeing service under an Indian prince but principally noted for his part in putting down the aftermath of the Indian Mutiny in 1857, actions he carried out with the zeal expected of his generation. Part of his response was to suggest a Bill for flaying alive, impaling, or burning the murderers of the women and children massacred at Delhi. Given this background and his robust Christian faith, Nicholson was surprised to be acclaimed as an incarnation of the Hindu God Brahma by a small sect that became known as the 'Nikalsainis'. This sect always remained obscure but significant enough to ensure that when Indian officials in the 1950s were taking down Nicholson's statute in Delhi, as part of a process of the removal of vestiges of British imperialism, an armed guard was posted in case the remnants of this sect would stage a protest. That statute now stands near the entrance to the Royal School, Dungannon.

A gentler Dungannon representative was Margaret Noble who met Swami Vivekananda in London in the 1890s and was so inspired that she moved to India, became a Hindu taking the name 'Nivedeta' (surely the first Hindu from Dungannon), and immersed herself in philanthropy and the Indian freedom struggle. On her death in 1911 she was praised by Tagore, the Indian Nobel Laureate, and her memorial in the Darjeeling Cremation Ground reads, 'Here reposes Sister Nivedeta who gave her all for India'.

In its earliest history, Ireland was the recipient of migrants who brought their distinct religious understanding with them. The first inter-faith encounters initiated by Irishmen and women occurred beyond our shores through the missionary outreach of monks such as Colum Cille and Columbanus in the sixth and seventh centuries. Whether the Irish saved civilisation is questionable but they did evangelise or re-evangelise much of Europe, spreading to Spain, France, Italy, Germany, Austria and as far east as Kiev. Examples include St Brendan (486-575) who is associated with boat journeys to the Feroe Islands, Greenland, the Azores, the Hebrides and Madeira. He potentially sailed as far as North America following the later Viking route of Iceland-Greenland-Newfoundland. These evangelists had a desire to see living faith in countries that formerly had been Christian but which, to some extent, had reverted to a form of paganism. Yet these monks were not crusading fanatics seeking to destroy all in their path and replace it with their particular form of Christianity. The general understanding of these monks was that Christianity could transform life and society but the pre-existing perspectives and values of pagan poets and seers were still important. The Celtic church was happy to baptise all that was good in cultures and to tolerate much that was not, both a strength and a weakness.

To some extent, this was the way Christianity had become established within Ireland and now a similar inclusive approach was being exported by these evangelists. The stereotypical condemnatory attitude of some of the nineteenth and twentieth century Northern Irish evangelists and Catholic dignitaries may well be foreign to Irish traditions. If a more inclusive approach is rediscovered in contemporary Ireland, this may allow a legitimate evangelical outreach to be combined with a claimed Irish welcome and acceptance of diversity that may sit more comfortably on tourist brochures than in Irish reality.

Chapter One has pointed to a small number of Irish being enslaved by Viking raiders and then sold on to Arab middlemen. The initial Irish experience of Islam could have been better but the major Christian-Muslim clash of civilisations during the eleventh to thirteenth centuries known as 'The Crusades' had very little Irish involvement. This was chiefly limited to the involvement of English knights who had Irish connections through the ownership of land or titles. After the Norman invasion of 1185 knights settled in Ireland and were expected to raise a small force of fighting men and participate in whatever was the current war, hence the involvement in the crusades. But they could only be called Irish in the most general of terms. There is record of an Irish delegation participating in a crusade council in Spain between 1095-96 and agreeing to send troops to fight the Muslims and reference to an unnamed Irish knight travelling with Godfrey de Bouillon. There are records of limited Scottish involvement and note should be taken that *Scoti* could mean either Scottish or Irish. But there is very little conclusive evidence that points to any significant Irish involvement.

However, Irish kings did go on pilgrimage to Rome and the Holy Land during this period, and these pilgrimages were often associated with small-scale limited crusades. The *Annals of Innisfallen* record the pilgrimage of Ua Cinn Fhaelad, King of the Deisi, to Jerusalem in 1080 while the *Annals of Loch Cé* record Aedh, son of Conchubhar Maenmhaighe, who died at the river Jordan in 1224 and Uaigharg Ua Ruairc, King of Breifne, who died in 1231 while travelling to the same river. One further intriguing connection was the role of Bernard of Clairveaux, a strident preacher for recruits for the twelfth century crusades, who was the friend and biographer of Malachy, Archbishop of Armagh (1132-1148). So there was an Irish dimension to this inter-faith turmoil that convulsed Europe and the Middle East for several hundred years, but only on the periphery. The con-

temporary Irish Christian and Irish Muslim relationship is not
overshadowed by the crusader legacy.

It was through interaction with the Indian sub-continent that
Islam and Hinduism first made a significant impact on the Irish.
During the era of the British Raj many Irishmen served as soldiers and administrators, the link going back to the earliest days
of British involvement on the Indian sub-continent. In the early
1600s the East India Company had built ships at Dundaniel on
the Bandon River, but left in 1615 due to local pressure over the
control of the dams and weirs that the English settlers had built.
An early Chairman of the Company was Lawrence Sullivan
from Cork and the Company policy of recruiting Catholics into
its militia, unlike the British army of the eighteenth century,
meant there were significant numbers of Irish soldiers serving in
its forces. The Bengal Army, part of the East India Company,
records that from 1825-1850 out of the 7620 recruits 47.9% were
Irish, whereas only 37.3% were English. Wolf Tone's brother,
William Henry Tone, served in this army, then later served in
the armies of Indian rulers, dying in battle in India. Irish soldiers
could also be found serving with the French army in India during the eighteenth century.

The Indian Civil Service was an attractive posting for the
younger sons of the Irish middle class and when competitive ex-
amination was introduced in 1855, rather than the previous system of patronage, the Irish proportion rose from 5% to 25%. To
train candidates for these exams Trinity College, Dublin introduced courses in Sanskrit and Arabic, Queen's College, Belfast
offered Indian language courses, and Indian history, geography
and law were all taught in Cork. In the 1890s seven of the eight
Indian provinces (including Burma) were run by Irishmen, but
Irish numbers dropped after this period due to the rising nationalism of southern Ireland and the policy of recruiting from
English public schools. Ulstermen were equally prominent, with
Lord John Lawrence from Londonderry serving as Viceroy from
1864-1869, being succeeded by the Earl of Mayo from 1869-1872.
Lawrence had at least two brothers who also served in India,

one dying during the siege of Luknow with 'No surrender!' his final words. Lord Dufferin, from Co Down, was Viceroy from 1884-1888, and during this period the Indian National Congress was formed as a multi religious group of Indian intellectuals striving for independence from Britain.

There was significant Irish involvement in one of the worst excesses of British rule in India. During a peaceful mass protest at Amritsar, the spiritual home of the Sikh community, General Reginald Dyer from Tipperary ordered the crowd to disperse. As his soldiers were blocking the only exit the crowd could not comply with this command and Dyer gave the order to open fire on the unarmed crowd, an action later defended by the Lieutenant Governor of Punjab, Sir Michael O'Dwyer of Cork. Officially 379 Indians were killed at Amritsar but the reality was probably closer to 600. Although recalled on half pay, Dyer was lauded in the British House of Commons by Tory members led by Dublin's Lord Carson and money was raised on his behalf. Queen Elizabeth II was later to apologise at Amritsar for this incident. Dyer also enforced the 'crawling order' whereby Indians were forced to crawl along a road where an English lady missionary had been assaulted. This law and its enforcement were significant factors in the radicalisation of Ghandi.

Of course, not all the Irish in India were soldiers or administrators. There were many Irish missionaries, most of whom took a very evangelical approach to Hinduism and Islam. Among the earliest was Father John Fennelly who came to Madras in 1842. One year earlier thirteen nuns had left Ireland to found a number of Loreto Convent schools. One of the most significant connections is through Mother Teresa of Calcutta who came to Ireland in 1928 to learn English from the Loreto sisters, travelled to Darjeeling to complete her training with the Loreto Sisters before settling in Calcutta. Irish Loreto sisters in India were also to educate relatives of the current Dalai Lama.

In 1838 two Irish Presbyterian ministers, James Glasgow and Alexander Kerr, were commissioned for missionary service in India, starting a long connection between that church and

Gujarat. The first convert was an influential Muslim, Abdur Rahman, a regular Hajj pilgrim who was baptised in 1843. Over the next hundred and fifty years Irish Presbyterianism sent a succession of missionaries to this area, mostly ministers, doctors and teachers. Given the climate, this was no easy mission and twenty-two were to give their lives in the evangelisation of this part of India. Mahatma Gandhi was among those positively influenced by this work, inviting the Irish Presbyterian Revd J. M. Lyle to teach English and Mark's gospel at his Ashram in 1920. It is interesting to speculate what influence this Irish Presbyterian may have had on Ghandi's developing inter-faith understanding.

Missionaries from the Irish Methodist and Anglican churches also had an important influence in this area. The first British Methodist missionaries to Asia included Revds James Lynch and George Erskine from Ireland. When the group's founder and leader, Revd Thomas Coke from Wales, died on the journey to the then Ceylon in 1813, Lynch from Donegal was appointed leader. After a couple of years in Ceylon Lynch moved on to Madras but eventually returned to work in Ireland. Since then there has been a regular succession of Irish Methodist missionaries working in Sri Lanka until the start of the twenty first century. Among notable Anglican contributions is that of Wellesley Bailey whose work, begun in the Punjab in the 1870s, has developed into the major international charity, 'The Leprosy Mission'. Presbyterian missionary work spread to China in 1869 and Malawi received its first Irish Presbyterian missionary in 1897, a country where Irish missionaries still serve. In the second half of the twentieth century Nepal has become a popular destination for Irish Protestant missionaries.

Illustrating the breadth of experience possible in the nineteenth century is the life of the Irish Methodist John McKenny. Born near Coleraine in 1788, McKenny became a Methodist minister and first served in the Cape Colony of South Africa from 1814-16. Not finding as much freedom to preach as he wanted from the colonial authorities, McKenny transferred to Ceylon where he worked from 1816-35 before being moved to New South Wales, remaining there until his death in 1847. Over a period of thirty three years McKenny was involved with followers of African tribal religions, Buddhism, Hinduism and Islam and extensively in Australia with followers of Aboriginal religion. One rural Ulsterman was able to encounter most world expressions of faith in the first half of the nineteenth century. The idea that Ireland has been immune to non-Christian religious influences in recent centuries should be seen as the myth that it is.

In the nineteenth century Irish Catholicism was mainly concerned with building Catholic Ireland and ministering to the spreading Irish diaspora in America, Australia and South Africa. So it was to be the twentieth century before the hugely impressive Irish Catholic missionary outreach took off. There was phenomenal missionary expansion in the first half of the twentieth century until half of Ireland's ten thousand priests were working abroad in the 1950s. In addition to serving the Irish diaspora, China and India had been popular destinations in the early twentieth century but it was in Africa that arguably the largest impact was made. The towering Irish figure was Bishop Joseph Shanahan. He had gone to what has become Nigeria in 1902 with a French missionary order and when appointed bishop he sought to recruit Irish priests and nuns to staff the parishes, schools and institutions of his vast diocese. This work developed into St Patrick's Missionary Society and through it many hundreds of Irish Catholic clergy have served in Nigeria. When the Biafran war erupted in 1967 there were hundreds of Irish Catholic missionaries caught up on both sides of the conflict, alongside a dozen Irish Methodist missionaries. The courageous response to this situation by a number of the Catholic missionaries kept this conflict front-page news in Ireland for its duration. It is not just in the twenty-first century that Africa has started to affect life in Ireland.

A very different Irish spiritual influence came through Annie Besant, born of Irish parents although raised in England. She was an influential member of the Theosophical Society that influenced Mahatma Ghandi during his years as a law student in London. It was founded in London in 1875 by Madam Blavatsky

as an 'eternal religion' that involved belief in karma, reincarnation and evolution, that all religions are part of the one religion
and that we can get in touch with our soul through dreams,
meditation and aligning ourselves with nature. Besant spent
forty years in India engaged in educational and political work,
founding the Central Hindu College of Benares in 1892 that developed into Benares Hindu University, and being elected
President of the Indian National Congress in 1917. Besant was
influenced by the independence struggle in Ireland and she was
imprisoned for some months in 1917, an action that helped to
radicalise Nehru. On her death Jawaharlal Nehru said of her,
'India owes a very deep debt of gratitude for all she did to enable India to find her own soul.'

Sharing a similar interest in Theosophy was William Judge.
Born in Dublin in 1851 he moved to New York where he became
a lawyer and founded the Theosophy Society in 1875. In 1884
Judge moved to India thinking it was to be permanent but ill
health forced him back to New York where he became editor of
The Path, the journal of the Theosophical Society. Judge went on
to publish a condensed version of the *Bhagavad-Gita*, and write
The Ocean of Theosophy. He was the leading light of American
theosophy for twenty years, associated with Madame Blavatsky
and Henry Olcott, and presided at the Theosophical Congress at
the World's Parliament of Religions in Chicago, 1893.

The political influence of Ireland on Nehru, who visited the
country at least twice during the Irish Home Rule agitation in
the early years of the twentieth century, has been well documented. Nehru was later to find himself in the hands of a very
sympathetic Irish jailer, a Captain Falvey, who was a former
pupil of Éamon De Valera, in Dehra Dun in 1932. Nehru made
several subsequent visits to Ireland after Indian independence.
A future Indian President was expelled from Ireland. V. V. Giri,
President of India from 1969-1974, studied law at University
College, Dublin, enrolling in 1913. He became involved with
Sinn Féin and trade union activism while in Dublin, and was deported for his republican sympathies in 1916. Presumably Giri is

the only future head of state to be deported from Ireland but given the current Irish enthusiasm for deporting asylum seekers this may not always be the case.

The Irish independence struggle was taken as an example by Ghandi who referred to parallels with the Irish situation numerous times in speeches. While there was certainly a political and spiritual influence from Ireland on India, it was also a two way process such as the cultural and religious impact on Ireland through the friendship between W. B. Yeats and Tagore. Yeats was strongly influenced by Hindu spitituality and wrote the 'Introduction' to Tagore's Nobel prize winning *Gitanjali*, and producing Tagore's play, *The Post Office*, in the Abbey Theatre in 1913. A further impact on Ireland was through the engineer and philanthropist Chester Beatty whose collection, eventually bequeathed to the Irish people, contained numerous Hindu and Muslim artefacts and writings.

Britain's colonial history was primarily for political and economic self-interest. At times missionaries were discouraged, such as in India, for potentially unsettling the inhabitants resulting in political difficulties. However Ireland's colonial history was a missionary history and so greater interest was taken in the religious habits of the native populations than taken by colonial administrators, for whom the indigenous religious understanding might become an interesting hobby but was not fundamental to his or her work. When the postman rode his bicycle up rural lanes to Irish farmhouses, he brought letters from missionaries in Asia, Africa, Australia and the Americas to their families back home. Nineteenth and early twentieth century Ireland knew all about the religious practices found in these lands, possibly better than contemporary populations in many other European nations. So when Ireland started to experience the arrival of small numbers of Muslims, Hindus and Sikhs in the 1950s, the religious expressions these people brought with them were not unknown to Irish people. They had been experiencing this as missionaries and reading about it as families for generations.

CHAPTER THREE

Ireland's Jewish Community

Between May 1899 and August 1902 the British-Israel Association excavated around the Hill of Tara, Co Meath until forced to stop by public pressure. The investigation had been planned for twenty-five years and was carried out by individuals who were convinced that the Anglo-Saxon people were descendants of the ten lost tribes of Israel and had a special, covenantal relationship with God. What they needed was proof and Tara was to uncover the links between Ireland, Britain, Israel and God. What were they confident of finding? Nothing less than the Ark of the Covenant described in Exodus 25:10-22.

Bizarre? Well, it does sound more like the plot from a Hollywood film but those involved included clergy, army officers, a member of the Royal Irish Academy and a member of the Royal Society of Antiquarians. British Israelite theory is based on John Sadler's *The Rights of the Kingdom* (1649) and John Wilson's *Our Israelite Origin* (1814). The beliefs are that the lost tribes of Israel wandered through western Europe before eventually settling in England as the Anglo-Saxon people. Old Testament prophecies are applied to British history, especially of the British Empire, and North America is included as the emigration of the Pilgrim Fathers continued the link. There is usually a degree of racism associated with these views and, while they are much less popular than formerly, there is still some support for these opinions amongst a small number of fundamentalist Christians in Northern Ireland. The excavation at Tara was taken so seriously that it was only widespread opposition led by such luminaries as Arthur Griffith, W. B. Yeats, Douglas Hyde and Maud Gonne that stopped their dig.

While this episode in the history of Tara is one of the more unusual, further details need not detain us. What it does open up is a possible interaction between Ireland and Israel going back to the mists or myths of time. It stands as a fascinating prelude to more documented inter-faith activity in Ireland, but imagine ... What if the Ark of the Covenant really *is* at Tara? Where does that place Ireland on a scale of inter-faith significance?

History of the Irish Jewish Community
Inter-faith encounter, whereby two or more faith communities live beside each other, interacting in the normal events of life including the religious sphere, really only began in Ireland with the arrival of the Jewish community. The first record of Jews visiting Ireland is in the *Annals of Innisfallen* that documents in the year 1079, 'Five Jews came over the sea with gifts to Tairdelbach [grandson of Brian Boru] and they were sent back again over the sea.' These Jews were probably from Rouen in France but clearly the Ireland of one hundred thousand welcomes was not yet in operation.

Before this date there are many suggestions as to connections between Ireland and the tribes of Israel but there is virtually no factual evidence to go on. Links have been claimed between the Stone of Destiny, *Lia Fáil*, taken from Tara in the fifth century to Scotland and subsequently taken by Edward I to Westminster Abbey, and a stone that was taken from the Temple Mount, Jerusalem, in 570BC. Tara itself is equated with Torah (Hebrew for 'law' and used to describe the first five books of the Bible), while the crowning and later freeing of a goat at the Puck Fair of Killorglin, Co Kerry is equated with the scapegoat of Leviticus chapter 16. Another tradition is of a granddaughter of Noah building an alternative ark and sailing to Ireland with fifty women and three men. How about considering that the 'Stone of Destiny' was accompanied to Ireland by Jeremiah who went on to establish Irish Brehon law based on the Ten Commandments? There is no solid factual basis for any of these legends although certain elaborate versions of these are still supported by those who follow the British Israelite view.

Moving to fact, there was a small Irish Jewish population in the twelfth and thirteenth centuries but they were expelled by royal decree on 18 July 1290. The next small influx to Ireland occurred after the Spanish and Portuguese expulsion of Jews in 1492 and a probable descendant was the Jewish Mayor of Youghal in 1555, William Annyas. However the history of Ireland and indeed the world could have been very different if the plan of James Harrington had been accepted. An associate of Oliver Cromwell, Harrington proposed solving Britain's perceived Irish and Jewish problems by turning Ireland into a national homeland for the Jews. Under this scheme Jewish populations from Britain and even Europe would have been settled in Ireland and, while no action was ever taken, it is fascinating to speculate whether two of the world's more intractable problems could actually have been solved if this plan had been enacted.

By the middle of the seventeenth century Jewish communal life was being established in Ireland, with records of a Sephardic Jew being granted the freedom of the city of Waterford in 1702. Numbers continued to grow slowly, a group of poor Ashkenazi Jews arriving at the start of the eighteenth century when much of Europe was at war. A synagogue at Crane Lane in Dublin had been established in 1660 although the population never publicly numbered more than a few dozen. For a while the Dublin Jewish community worshipped in a building in St Mary's Abbey, near Capel Street, that had formerly been owned by a Presbyterian group and it subsequently became known as the 'Jews Temple'. Due to restrictive laws and public opposition, some Jews may have kept their religion secret upon arrival in Ireland. A parishioner of St Michan's Church in Dublin, David Sollom, lived as a Christian but on burial in 1682 was recorded as 'a quondam Jewish merchant'. In Northern Ireland the first Jewish record dates from 1652. In that year there was at least one Jew in residence in Belfast by the name of Manuel Lightfoot, a tailor, and the 1771 census record of a Jewish butcher indicated the presence of a reasonably sized community.

Attitudes varied but European Christians generally looked on Jews with disdain and there is no evidence to show that Ireland was any different, although the small Jewish numbers never allowed them to be a significant perceived economic threat to the established population, as was the case in some other parts of Europe. Between 1743 and 1748 four bills were introduced into the Irish Parliament to facilitate the naturalisation of foreign-born Jews, but all were rejected. Acts passed in 1780 and 1783 granting aliens the right to naturalisation expressly excluded Jews. The Irish Naturalisation Act of 1783 was repealed in 1816 and from then on Jews could be naturalised in Ireland. It could be that Irish attitudes reflected the views of the British ascendancy more than containing any uniquely Irish factor. Yet against that, the history of the Vatican's historic attitude to the Jews is well documented as one containing a significant measure of aggression and discrimination and this Vatican influence on Irish attitudes cannot be discounted. While under the Penal Laws Roman Catholic influence over the rulers of Ireland was not that significant, still the Roman Catholic community, as a majority in Ireland, may have helped to diffuse this attitude in the general psyche. Our reading of history sometimes reflects only the views of the ruling class, when the view of the 'ordinary citizen' could have been very different.

Some Christians considered the Jewish population as ripe for evangelism and chief among these was the eccentric Bishop Robert Clayton of Clogher (1695-1758). When not throwing riotous parties at his St Stephen's Green, Dublin residence Bishop Clayton found time in 1751 to publish *An Impartial Enquiry into the Time of the Coming of the Messiah* as an aid to Jewish evangelism. There were a number of baptisms of Jews associated with their marriage to Christians, a recurrent issue for the Jewish community in Ireland, and one that was to be paralleled in the experience of the Protestant community in the Republic of Ireland during most of the twentieth century. There were also a small number of conversions that appear to have been for purely spiritual reasons. Abraham Jacobs had been a salaried official of the Dublin synagogue and was baptised in St Peter's Church in Aungier St, Dublin on 2 June 1706. The Archbishop of Dublin published an account of this conversion (as also happened after the conversion of John Meirs in 1709) as an aid to evangelising the Irish Jews. The Jewish community responded by taking Jacob's family abroad so that he could not make them Christians.

From this we can deduce that the eighteenth and nineteenth century Irish Christian attitude to the Jewish community was one of general intolerance coupled with some evangelistic activity, but both in a very mild way compared to the experiences of Jewish communities living in ghettos in Europe, including the Vatican states. Ireland never had Jewish ghettos and while there were certain areas where Jews predominated, this was the action of an immigrant community living together for mutual support rather than forced by the ostracising of a wider community. 'The Liberator' Daniel O'Connell was able to claim on 11 September 1829 that Ireland is 'the only country I know of unsullied by one act of persecution of the Jews'. While that is not fully supported by historical evidence, it does illustrate the relatively peaceful nature of the Irish Jewish experience in comparison to the rest of Europe, although the overwhelming factor must be the largely insignificant number of Jews resident. In 1816 Dublin had just nine Jews living within the city boundaries. Generally speaking Ireland was a country to escape to, not flee from.

Among those who advocated tolerance of the Jews was Archbishop Richard Whateley, Anglican Archbishop of Dublin, a strong supporter of Catholic emancipation who spoke eloquently in the House of Lords on 1 August 1833 in favour of the Jews' Relief Bill. Sparked by the inability of the Jewish Lionel de Rothschild to take his seat in the English House of Commons due to his unwillingness to take the oath as a Christian, the Dublin paper *The Inspector* argued for religious toleration in its 14 September 1850 edition.

Around 1845, a Daniel Jaffe, a merchant from Hamburg, visited Belfast for the purpose of establishing contacts for the purchase of linen goods and within the next decade, there were three linen houses functioning in Belfast by the name of Jaffe Brothers, George Betzold & Company and Moore & Weinberg. In 1845 the *Belfast Protestant Journal* recorded that Dr Morris Jacob Raphael was prevented from speaking about Judaism by a mob outside the Commercial Building in Belfast. Raphael got a better reception in North America and was the first Jewish cleric invited to open the American House of Representatives with prayer in 1860.

By the year 1869 the number of Jewish residents in Belfast was still only twenty-one but a synagogue was built in 1871 in Great Victoria Street. In 1898 a Jewish elementary school was established and in 1907 a school was opened on Belfast's Cliftonville Road. Daniel Jaffe's son, Otto, was elected a Belfast City Councillor in 1894 and then Lord Mayor in 1899 and 1904, being knighted after his first term. From a Jewish background although a baptised Christian, Gustav Wolff came from Hamburg in 1834 and with a colleague, Richard Harland, founded the famous Belfast shipbuilders bearing their names in 1862.

It was anti-Semitic religious legislation in Czarist Russia that significantly increased the Irish Jewish population. The introduction by the Russian Parliament of the 'May Laws' in 1882 caused large sections of Russian Jewry to attempt to leave. These were temporary measures issued under Czar Alexander III, although they were to last for thirty years. These laws restricted the ability of Jews to live outside of towns, to buy or sell property and forbade business activity on Sundays or Christian holidays. Between 1881 and 1905 approximately 100,000 Russian Jews came to Britain. Those who came to Ireland were mostly peasants from Lithuania who spoke no English and had few contacts among the existing small Irish Jewish community. Most travelled overland across Europe to England before making their way to Ireland, searching for opportunities of employment and especially to establish themselves in business. A number achieved this in a very short period of time, largely in the food, clothing and furniture industries. The Irish Jewish population

rose from 1,779 in 1891 to 3,769 ten years later and, while far
from numerous, there were visible populations of several hundred in Dublin, Belfast and Cork.

In Dublin in 1901 there were Jews employed as drapers (261),
peddlers (223) and tailors (72) and these increasing numbers
made the Jewish traders an economic threat, albeit a small one,
to the existing Christian population, provoking the start of relatively serious anti-Semitic activity in Ireland. In October 1886
posters were distributed throughout Dublin warning the population to do no business with the newly arrived Jews although
the *Freeman's Journal* of 23 October 1886 considered this the
work of a tiny number of fanatics. In any case, agitation soon
died away. In the *Irish Catholic* of July 1893 a Roman Catholic
priest argued in a letter that the Jews were being expelled from
Russia for immoral behaviour while the Dublin Recorder made
anti-Jewish comments in his sentencing. In October 1892 Mr
Frederick Falkiner QC claimed of a Jew that 'These fellows
would swear anything', while in January 1902, when sentencing
a Jew for breaking windows, he said 'You are a specimen of your
race and nation that cause you to be hunted out of every country'. However, the Adelaide Road Synagogue, opened in 1892,
had received financial support from the wider community and a
number of Christians attended its opening. In 1910 Mr Justice
Kenny spoke of the contribution that Jews had and were making
to Irish life and that anti-Jewish attitudes reflected on the holder
of those views rather than the Jews.

Yet in both Cork and Limerick, around the end of the nineteenth and the start of the twentieth century, events stand out
that show a significant level of anti-Semitism and in two cases
the problems were sparked by Christians with a religious motivation, although the underlying factors were almost certainly
economic.

In Cork a Jewish congregation, existing from around 1725,
had died out by the end of the eighteenth century but revived
again in 1881 with the arrival of a few Lithuanian Jews. The
newcomers received a warm welcome and a Presbyterian minis-

ter, Revd Matthew Kerr, helped them establish themselves and, with others, collected the necessary funds to purchase a burial ground for their community. In 1888 two foreigners known as Katz, wrongly perceived as belonging to the Cork Jewish community, established a business to import cheap furniture made by American convicts. The 'Cork Trades Union' started to agitate against them and persecution was threatened against the Jewish community. It was only through intervention by Charles Stewart Parnell, then leader of the Irish Party, to the mayor of Cork that the Jewish community was exonerated. A more serious incident occurred in May 1894 after a series of open-air Protestant meetings that were resented by the Catholic population. After a Sunday afternoon meeting a newly arrived Lithuanian Jew was mistaken for one of the preachers and assaulted by a mob. Despite police intervention many Jews were then attacked, homes stoned and one Jewish shop burnt. The Jewish community had no part in the original problem caused by the Protestant preachers but suffered despite their innocence. This occurred during an era when anti-Semitism was increasing throughout Europe.

Limerick had only two resident Jews in 1871 but the subsequent arrival of about twenty Lithuanian families swelled the numbers, most being employed in selling books and pictures. On Holy Thursday 1884 a maid had observed her Jewish employer slaughtering a chicken in the Jewish ritual way. This was mistaken for an act of cruelty and a mob stoned the home of Lieb Siev on Easter Sunday morning, injuring his wife and child. Two of the mob were eventually sentenced to a month's imprisonment with hard labour and the small Jewish community was vindicated of any wrongdoing. As the community grew to around 130 further small incidents occurred, with two Jews assaulted in August 1892 and the home of Moses Leone stoned on 24 November 1896.

By the start of the twentieth century many of the Jewish community were employed as travelling drapers or milk vendors, collecting their money weekly and providing a very useful service to the poor of the local community. However, without much warning, on 12 January 1904 a sermon by the Redemptorist Fr John Creagh denounced the Jewish population in dramatic terms. The Jews were accused of extorting money from the community and being prepared to kidnap and kill Christian children, a commonplace accusation against Jews in this era. Arthur Griffith, leader of Sinn Féin, supported Creagh, contending that the Irish poor needed freeing from international moneylenders, but others such as the economist Fred Ryan were prepared to speak out on behalf of the Jews. Michael Davitt of the United Irish League denounced the child killing accusation, protesting 'as an Irishman and a Christian, against this spirit of barbarous malignity being introduced into Ireland' in a letter to *Freeman's Journal*, 18 January 1904. Davitt, as a journalist, had written about Jewish persecution in 1903 in *Within the Pale: The True Story of Anti- Semitic Persecutions in Russia*.

It would appear that Creagh was reacting against the recent expulsion of two hundred Redemptorists from France, supposedly after Jewish agitation. A further factor was the encouragement of Limerick businessmen who were becoming concerned at the current and potential economic impact of the Jewish traders. In subsequent sermons Creagh advocated the avoidance of business with the Jewish community and a refusal to repay debts. Some Protestants responded by raising funds for the thirty-five Jewish families and the problem escalated. The Jewish business practice of collecting money weekly was a well-established custom employed by virtually all traders in Limerick and elsewhere in the early twentieth century and still occasionally found in rural Ireland today. Jewish homes and businesses were attacked and the boycott of Jewish businesses intensified, forcing many into poverty. Some Catholics denounced these actions, for instance a letter by 'Galatea' in the *Limerick Daily Express* of 14 April 1904 considered that, 'Such narrow-minded bigotry does not express the sentiments of Catholic Ireland.' The courts punished those convicted of assault although *The Limerick Leader* of 15 April 1904 records the case of a fifteen year old boy being sentenced to one month in prison for stoning Rabbi Levin by commenting on the harshness of the sentence and that there 'was not a single Catholic magistrate at the hearing of the case'.

The boycott lasted for two years and drove 80 of the 120 members of the Jewish community away from Limerick. The Bishop of Limerick, Dr Edward Thomas O'Dwyer, appears to have disapproved of Creagh's actions but had little direct influence over Creagh since the latter was not a diocesan priest. O'Dwyer took little action whereas his Anglican counterpart, Bishop Bunbury, spoke strongly against Creagh at the Church of Ireland Synod that year. Rabbi Levin called with Bishop O'Dwyer on 19 January 1904 but was only met by the bishop's secretary. The superior general of the Redemptorists, Fr Mathias Raus, visited Limerick on 22 July 1904 but refused to meet Rabbi Levin.

Whether Creagh's superiors ultimately approved or disapproved of his actions is hard to judge. Creagh was transferred first to Belfast and then to the Philippines, leaving Ireland on 12 May 1906. He died at the Redemptorist Monastery of St Gerard in Wellington, New Zealand in January 1947.

These events, known as the 'Limerick Pogrom', pale into insignificance when compared to contemporary pogroms in Russia and subsequently in countries under Nazi occupation. There is a case for arguing that the use of *pogrom*, an emotive word, is unjustified as a description of these events. Indeed this point was argued by the Redemptorist Fr Bailey in letters to the *Irish Times* of 3 August 1984 and 6 September 1984. In Limerick no-one was killed or even seriously injured, although that should not minimise the impact on the Jewish community as most were forced to leave through intimidation or the resultant poverty. The events in Limerick 1904-1906 are normally considered as the worst case of anti-Semitism in Irish history and while economic factors were crucial, there was certainly an inter-religious element present. While smaller Protestant denominations were not involved, their general indifference to the case is of note. For example there was no published Irish Methodist comment on the events of Limerick 1904-06. The Methodist paper, *The Irish Christian Advocate*, made no reference to the events and in the same period regularly supported missions who sought to convert Jews. There was an awareness of international problems that Jews were facing, with the persecution of Russian Jews denounced in editions on 9 September 1904, 4 August 1905, 24 November 1905, 1 December 1905, 22 December 1905, 2 March 1906 and 9 March 1906. However a charge of anti-Semitism cannot be laid against the paper and on 2 February 1906 an article appeared complimenting the Jewish community in America for their industry and progress, although on 1 April 1904 an article condemned immigration commenting that 'the offscouring of continental cities is pouring into London, Glasgow and Belfast'. On 5 October 1906 The British Society for the Propagation of the Gospel Among the Jews held a service in Donegall Square Methodist Church, Belfast where the speaker declared that the Jews 'had been persecuted in every Christian country with the exception of Ireland'. By this date the Limerick Jewish community had been economically destroyed and almost all had left the city. The only reference to a boycott in Limerick during this period was a letter in the 22 July edition from a Limerick Methodist doctor complaining of a cab driver regularly refusing to accept him for religious and political reasons.

James Joyce's Leopold Bloom is a fascinating creation and shows a tolerance in the midst of anti-Semitism. Joyce's Dublin Jew, a central character in *Ulysses*, was an ethnically Jewish foreigner and a convert to Christianity who faces up to the insults his race receives with dignity and is the opposite of the picture that Creagh had drawn in 1904. Joyce was responding to the racism and anti-semitism that was prevalent in Irish and British life and attacking the notion of Ireland's *céad míle fáilte*:

> Ireland, they say, has the honour of being the only country which never prosecuted the Jews. Do you know that? And do you know why? ... – Because she never let them in, Mr Deasy said solemnly.

This statement arguably was to prove a correct assessment of Irish foreign policy over the twenty-five years following Joyce's penning of those lines.

The Irish state proved its willingness to accommodate the Jewish minority by part financing Zion Schools to the extent of £4,000 out of a total cost of £12,000, the school being opened on 25 March 1934. The Jewish method of ritual slaughter of animals, *Shehitah*, was accepted by Dublin Corporation and Ireland's Jews escaped the persecutions widespread throughout mainland Europe in the 1930s and 1940s. Whether the smaller scale anti-Semitism that did exist in Ireland was due to a tolerance among the Irish, or more due to demographic factors, is hard to determine. In the 1930s when Ireland had about 4,000 Jews, Poland had 3,000,000, Germany 500,000, and Britain 300,000. Arguably the level of intolerance in Ireland was respectively not much less than elsewhere. Thirty-five families in Limerick had produced a two-year campaign of opposition. If there had been 50,000 Jews in Ireland it is to be presumed, on the available evidence, that there would have been a significant level of persecution, although not on the scale of the worst excesses in Europe.

During the Second World War three main factors show the level of anti-Semitism at this time. Firstly, certain Catholic publications had an anti-Semitic slant, secondly, the presence of the 'Blueshirts' and, thirdly, the response of de Valera's government to requests for Jewish immigration.

Denis Fahey, Professor of Theology at Kimmage, Dublin repeated accusations that were becoming rife in Europe, namely, that communism and Judaism were linked in a conspiracy to overthrow the existing world order. Writing in popular Catholic periodicals and especially in *The Mystical Body of Christ in the Modern World* (1935), Fr Edward Cahill, a Jesuit who founded 'Catholic Action' in 1927, made similar claims of Jewish plans to control international finance and media. These views helped to underpin the general anti-Semitic attitude in Ireland but were not taken seriously by de Valera. Other notable Irish anti-Semites included Oliver St John Gogarty whose 1937 memoirs

As I was Going Down Sackville Street: A Phantasy in Fact resulted
in him being fined £900 in a libel case taken by the Harris family,
leading members of the Irish Jewish community. Oliver Flanagan,
one time Defence Minister, made several anti-Semitic attacks in
the Dáil, notably on 9 July 1943.

General Eoin O'Duffy, sacked in 1933 from his position as
Commissioner of the Garda Síochána, founded the Blueshirts
who were modelled on Mussolini's combination of fascism,
Catholicism and nationalism. Associated with Fine Gael, they
rejected the charge of anti-Semitism, with the Presbyterian
Ernest Blythe of Fine Gael assuring Arthur Newman of the
Jewish community that the party would never discriminate between citizens on the basis of religion. The Blueshirt movement
was only transient, unlike its equivalents in Italy and Germany,
and while enjoying significant popular support for a period, it
did not prove enduring. Equally short-lived was 'The Irish
Christian Front', founded by a former Blueshirt, Paddy Belton,
on 21 August 1936 to fight for Franco in Spain. Frank Ryan, formerly of the IRA, fought with a few others for the Spanish com-
munists, but the majority support in the Republic of Ireland was
for Franco who received significant Catholic support in Spain.
Paddy Belton had made a number of anti-Semitic remarks in the
Dáil and Dublin Corporation, causing Rabbi Herzog to correspond with Cardinal Joseph MacRory but, like the Blueshirts, this
movement did not gain lasting popular support.

Of more significance was Charles Bewley, appointed Irish
ambassador in Berlin in August 1933, who quickly proved to be
in support of the current German policies, attending the Nazi
Party annual rallies at Nurenburg when many of his diplomatic
colleagues refused such invitations. Bewley was later to write a
rather partisan biography of Hermann Goering in which he suggested, 'National Socialism, whatever might be its defects,
should be upheld by the Western Powers as the strongest, perhaps the only, force which could prevent the spread of the
Communist Empire over half Europe.'

Others with similar views included the Irish novelist Francis

Stuart who lectured at Berlin University and whose novels, such as *Julie, The Great Squire, Women and God*, and *In Search of Love* contained anti-Semitic scenes. He broadcast German propaganda to Ireland from Berlin during 1942-44 and wrote scripts for William Joyce, better known as 'Lord Haw-Haw'. In 1945 the anti-Semitic Malachy Conlon was elected from South Armagh to the Northern Ireland parliament.

During this period a similar debate was ongoing within the Irish American community. In the late 1920s and 1930s Fr Charles Coughlin of Detroit, one of the first 'shock jocks' of radio, had an audience peaking at 40 million who listened avidly to his increasingly anti-Semitic and pro Nazi opinions. Monsignor John Ryan was one Irish American priest who denounced Coughlin's populist views, at a time when the hierarchy were wary of tackling him. Coughlin was eventually silenced after the USA's entry into World War II when the Justice Department complained to the archbishop that Coughlin's views were against America's interests.

In 1937 the Chief Rabbi of Ireland, Dr Isaac Herzog, left Ireland to become the Chief Rabbi of Palestine, perhaps the most sensitive inter-faith position in the Jewish world. At this time of European turmoil fuelled by the aggressive policies of Nazism in Germany, Ireland was faced with calls to accept Jewish refugees who were fleeing persecution in countries as varied as Germany, Austria, Poland, Romania and Hungary. At the Evian refugee conference, called by President Roosevelt to consider how to deal with the increasing numbers of stateless Jews, Ireland expressed concern at the problem but offered little practical help, citing financial constraints. The Irish Department of Justice was very reluctant to grant any entry visas and only direct intervention by de Valera, in particular cases, allowed concessions. An example is the significant number of Jewish doctors and dentists who wished to come and practice in Ireland, many of whom were Austrian Jews who could see in 1938 how the situation in their country was likely to develop. The Ministry for Industry and Commerce felt that economic reasons should prevent this but the insular Irish perspective may have been more significant.

On 4 December 1938 'The Irish Co-ordinating Committee for the Relief of Christian Refugees from Central Europe' was launched. This group represented Roman Catholic, Anglican, Quaker and Jewish interests and while there was government co-operation with this body, visas for refugees would still only be issued where it could be proved that an individual would be of economic benefit to Ireland. The Quakers, despite their very small numbers, proved one of the most active constituents of this group. Their international centre in Vienna proved an effective conduit for refugees and many of the small number who came were housed in Quaker homes and attended the Quaker school at Newtown Park, Waterford, others attending Wesley College and The High School, both in Dublin. During the period 1933 to 1939, when Ireland was proving a virtually impossible country for Jews to settle in, Britain accepted 42,000 Jews, USA 85,000, France 30,000 and Latin America 85,000. In Millisle the Belfast Jewish community established a home for Jewish refugees and about eighty, mostly children, lived there. The children were educated and many of the boys joined the British forces when old enough to enlist.

During World War II many members of Ireland's Jewish community served in the British forces or the Irish Local Defence Force such as the Dubliner, Dr Bethel Solomon's sons, Michael and Bethel jnr, both doctors, who served in the Royal Air Force and the British Army respectively. The only Irish born Jew to die in the holocaust was Esther Steinberg of Dublin who moved to Belgium upon marriage in 1937. She was to die in Auschwitz. Many European Jews who had family links with Ireland were murdered after requests for visas to Ireland were refused or delayed. The charge of institutional anti-Semitism, albeit of a relatively mild form when compared with much of Europe, is hard to refute.

At this time the Irish Jewish community was able to influence, to some extent, government policy, chiefly through the intervention of the Jewish TD, Robert Briscoe. The Roman Catholic Archbishop of Dublin from 1940, Dr John Charles McQuaid, also helped to combat any rising tide of anti-Semitism in Dublin.

During the war years, when the generally accepted figure of holocaust victims is approximately 6,000,000, the Republic of Ireland accepted an unknown number of Jewish refugees but it may have been as little as sixty. During the same dates USA accepted about 250,000 refugees and Palestine 150,000. It was not a proud period in Irish history and in 1995, during the Holocaust Memorial, An Taoiseach John Bruton apologised to the Irish Jewish community for the Irish government's response during the Holocaust.

The 2 May 1945 visit of de Valera to the German ambassador to pay condolences after Hitler's death adds to the charge of anti-Semitic action. There is no evidence that de Valera had any anti-Semitic attitudes – his close friendship with Rabbi Herzog would tend to disprove any such accusations – but his 2 May visit showed, at best, a huge indifference to the feelings of the Irish Jewish community. It is hard to gauge exactly the motives for this widely condemned action that has remained part of de Valera's legacy

Yet there were alternatives to this anti-Semitic history. Monsignor Hugh O'Flaherty from Cahirciveen, Co Kerry studied for the priesthood in Rome and remained working in the Vatican after his ordination. O'Flaherty witnessed the rising tide of anti-Semitism in 1930s Rome and was fully aware of the neutrality agreement between the Vatican and Hitler whereby Hitler respected Vatican neutrality and the Vatican agreed not to interfere with German actions. For O'Flaherty this meant that if he were caught helping Roman Jews the Vatican would not support him. Undeterred O'Flaherty set about providing safety in Vatican buildings and other church-owned property for Jews, gypsies and others trying to escape from Fascist authorities. When Mussolini's regime fell and German troops took over, O'Flaherty used the same safe houses and escape roots to aid

Italian prisoners of war. Jewish authorities considered that he helped approximately 4,000 Jews to escape and O'Flaherty was hailed as a war hero. The State of Israel named him a 'Righteous Gentile', their highest award to a non-Jew.

The last fifty years have witnessed a mature Irish Jewish community being eroded, largely due to emigration to Israel, USA and Britain. Numbers peaked at about 6,000 in the late 1950s but have reduced to only 200 in Belfast and around 1500 in Dublin at the start of the third millennium. Anti-Semitic actions have almost disappeared, and those that have occurred have usually been as a result of individual action rather than by communities or groups. The anti-Semitic views of Mayor Coughlan of Limerick in 1970 were challenged by Gerald Goldberg and by Jim Kemmy of Coughlan's own Labour Party. Kemmy left the Labour Party in 1971 due to its failure to discipline Coughlan. Kemmy went on to found the Democratic Socialist Party and represent Limerick in Dáil Éireann from 1981-82. Kemmy again defended the Limerick Jewish community in letters to the *Irish Times* on 23 August 1984 and 18 September 1984 during a dispute with Fr Michael Bailey of the Redemptorists. When a petrol bomb was thrown at the Cork Synagogue in 1983 the Jewish community was heartened by the support the Christian community gave and considered the attack more a protest against the policies of Israel than against the Jews of Cork. Six years earlier the Cork Corporation had voted in Gerald Goldberg, a Jew, as mayor.

The presence of the leaders of Ireland at Jewish occasions has become the norm. When Immanuel Jakobovits was installed as Chief Rabbi of Ireland on 15 February 1949 the celebration dinner was attended by the Taoiseach, John Costello. Ireland's first Jewish Civic Service took place in Adelaide Road Synagogue in 1956 to mark the election of Robert Briscoe as Dublin's first Jewish Lord Mayor. In 1984 the installation of President Hillery saw official participation by the Chief Rabbi for the first time, with the Jewish community recording it as 'another remarkable reflection of the position of the Jewish community in Ireland as a whole'. President Hillery visited the Jewish Home for the Aged in 1990 and President Robinson opened an extension there in 1992.

President Robinson caused some confusion when she was to attend the installation of the Chief Rabbi, Gavin Broder in Terenure Synagogue in 1998. Women sit in the gallery but this was considered potentially disrespectful to the President. The compromise was that President Robinson sat in the gallery between her husband and her military aide, as if on a reviewing stand. The Chief Rabbi is consulted by the Taoiseach, as are Christian leaders, with regard to major political developments such as before the signing of the Anglo-Irish Agreement of 1985. The Chief Rabbi is present at all major state occasions and a frequent visitor to the Mansion House and Áras An Uachtaráin when foreign dignitaries are present.

As a community fully involved in the life of Ireland, the Jewish community, despite their small numbers, have shared in Ireland's recent conflict. Simone Chetrit, a French Jew working in Ireland as an *au pair*, was killed in the Dublin bomb explosions of 17 May 1974 and the Belfast Jewish community, situated largely in north Belfast, have been witnesses to some of Ulster's worst sectarian excesses.

WHAT IS THE IRISH JEWISH FAITH?

Around 2,000 years ago a non-Jew told Hillel, a famous Jewish teacher, that he would convert to Judaism if Hillel could teach him the whole of the Torah in the time he could balance on one leg. Hillel replied, 'What is hateful to yourself, do not do to your neighbour. That is the whole Torah; the rest is just commentary.'

The Founder
It is harder to point to a founder of Judaism compared to other religions such as Buddhism or Islam. Judaism draws it roots in God's creative purpose and his election of a covenant people rather than a charismatic founder or saviour. Through a series of patriarchs, prophets, kings and judges Judaism has been main-

tained and renewed as a living faith for a particular ethnic community.

Development

The ancient history of the Jewish community is recorded in what Christians call the Old Testament. It is a story of a community struggling to maintain independence from a variety of relatively local and then international powers, finally disappearing as a sovereign people during the Roman era. More recently much of the community strength was found in eastern Europe, partly due to opposition and persecution in many western European states. A series of pogroms culminated in the Nazi attempt to destroy the community in the 1930s and 1940s resulting in approximately six million deaths in the Holocaust or *Shoah*. Israel was established in 1948 as a Jewish homeland and, despite political opposition from the displaced Palestinian community and neighbouring Arab states, Israel exists as a visible representation of the Jewish people and faith.

Differences

Judaism comes in many varieties but in Ireland it is experienced largely in Orthodox and Progressive forms. The Chief Rabbi of Ireland is from the Orthodox community and acts in a representative role for the whole Jewish community. It would be fair to say that sometimes the Progressive community is marginalised within Ireland. Being the minority of a very small minority is sometimes an uncomfortable place to occupy.

Beliefs

Jews combine two different-sounding ideas of God in their beliefs: that God is an all-powerful being who is quite beyond human ability to understand or imagine, and that God is here with us, caring about each individual as a parent cares for his/her child. A great deal of Jewish study deals with the creative power of two apparently incompatible ideas of God.

Worship

The Jewish Sabbath begins at sunset on Friday and lasts until sunset on Saturday. For observant Jews to ensure that the Sabbath is different, all work in preparation for the Sabbath must be finished before sunset on Friday. People generally dress smartly for Sabbath and go to considerable trouble to ensure that everything is in place to obey the commandment to make the Sabbath a delight. Sabbath candles are lit and there are special Sabbath blessings, prayers, songs and readings. It is traditional for the whole family to attend worship on Saturday although Irish Jews are no different to Jews elsewhere in a growing secularism.

The synagogue or *shul* is a place of study and community centre as well as the main Jewish place of worship. In Orthodox synagogues men and women sit separately, whereas in Progressive synagogues men and women generally sit together. Synagogue services can be led by a rabbi, a cantor or a member of the congregation. Traditional Jewish worship requires a *minyan* or quorum of ten adult males to take place. The synagogue in Cork is only open on High Holy days because of a lack of ten males. For these occasions Jewish males come from Dublin or England to enable the services to be held. In an Orthodox synagogue the service will be conducted by men in ancient Hebrew with congregational and/or choir singing. The alternative is in a Progressive synagogue where the service will be at least partly in English, often there is a choir and instruments and men and women can sit together. Women can participate as fully as men and women Rabbis are permitted.

In Orthodox synagogues the *Bimah* or raised place is always in the middle of the hall whereas in a progressive synagogue it is often directly in front of the Ark. In front of the *Bimah* is a lectern where the Torah is placed for readings.

Jewish men always wear hats when they are saying prayers which mention God's name, observant Jewish men wearing some sort of hat almost all the time, normally a small round cap called a *yarmulke* (Yiddish) or a *kippah* (Hebrew). Men over the age of thirteen often wear a *Tallit* or prayer shawl for morning prayer, the fringes (called *tzitzit*) on the edges reminding the wearer to observe God's commandments as instructed in the *Shemah*, one of the most sacred prayers.

Each synagogue contains an Ark or cupboard where the Torah scrolls containing the text of the Hebrew Bible are kept. The Ark is named after the wooden chest that held the stone tablets of the Covenant that God gave to Moses on Mount Sinai and the Hebrew words of the Ten Commandments are usually written somewhere above the ark. At the proper moment in the service the Ark is ceremonially opened and the Torah scroll is carried in procession to the reading desk, unrolled to the reading chosen for the day and laid on the reading desk. Normally the congregation stands whenever the doors of the ark are open. An Eternal Light (*Ner Tamid*) hangs above the Ark. This light is kept burning as a symbol of God's presence and to represent the pillar of fire that guided the Jewish people on their journey through the wilderness.

Jews are supposed to pray three times a day: morning, afternoon, and evening. Much Jewish prayer consists in reciting the written services aloud in synagogue. Observant Jews will say a blessing over everything they eat or drink, and in the face of many natural events, to acknowledge that God is involved in all parts of life.

There are currently six synagogues in Ireland. Three Orthodox synagogues are found in south Dublin, one in north Belfast and one in Cork. A Progressive/Liberal synagogue is found in the Rathgar area of south Dublin.

Living the faith
Jews believe that God choose them in order to set an example of holiness and ethical behaviour to the world. Jewish life is very much the life of a community and there are many activities that Jews must do as a community. Judaism is a faith of action and Jews believe people should be judged by the way they live their faith rather than by the intellectual content of their beliefs.

Orthodox Jews believe that a Jew is someone who is the child of a Jewish mother, and who has not adopted another faith. Progressive Jews are prepared to accept as Jewish someone who has a Jewish father or mother.

While the Jewish-run food shops have largely disappeared from Ireland, kosher food can currently be purchased in Super Valu, Churchtown and Bretzels Bakery, Lennox Street, both in Dublin and Safeways supermarket on the Shore Road and Ewing's Fish shop on the Shankill Road, both in Belfast.

Holy days

The Jewish calendar is a combined moon and sun calendar, unlike the conventional Western (or Gregorian) calendar. Consequently, Jewish festivals move about the Western calendar from year to year. The High Holy Days come in autumn, at the start of the month of Tishri. This is the most spiritual period of the year for Jews, a time for looking back on the year just passed, and for taking action to get right with God and with other people. It runs from Rosh Hashanah for ten days until Yom Kippur. These High Holy festivals include:

1. Rosh Hashanah: the New Year festival and commemorates the creation of the world.

2. Days of Awe or Repentance: the ten days between Rosh Hashanah and Yom Kippur during which everyone gets a chance to repent.

3. Yom Kippur: the most sacred and solemn day of the Jewish year which brings the Days of Repentance to a close with a twenty-five hour fast.

The Pilgrimage Festivals commemorate the journey of the Jewish People from Egypt to the Holy Land and mark the dates in Temple times when Jews made pilgrimage to the Temple in Jerusalem for sacrifice. They are:

1. Passover or Pesach: a spring festival marking the escape from captivity in Egypt.

2. Shavuot: marks the time when the Jews received God's laws at Mount Sinai.

3. Sukkot or The Feast of Tabernacles: commemorates the years that the Jews spent in the desert on their way to the Promised Land and how God provided for them.

Other Festivals include:

1. Purim: marking the defeat of an attempt to wipe out the Jews by Haman during the reign of Xerxes.

2. Hanukkah, or the Festival of Lights: marking the restoration of the temple by the Maccabees in 164 BCE. Hanukkah is celebrated at roughly the same time as Christmas.

3. Tish B'av is the ninth day of the Jewish month of Av that usually falls in July or August in Ireland. It is a solemn occasion because it commemorates a series of tragedies that have befallen the Jewish people over the years, many of which have coincidentally happened on this day, most especially two successive destructions of the Temple.

Adaptation and Contribution to Ireland
Ireland's Jews have contributed to Ireland's social and cultural life far beyond what their numbers justify. This claim is often made by some of the Protestant denominations; it is especially true in the case of the Jewish community. Jews have represented Ireland at a number of sports, such as Bethel Solomons, capped ten times for Ireland at rugby between 1908 and 1910, going on to become a selector. He records the fascinating inter-faith understanding of an Irish rugby supporter during his playing career. When Ireland beat Scotland a bar room conversation reputedly went 'That was a grand Irish team that won today.' The reply was, 'Call that an Irish team with fourteen Protestants and one bloody Jew?'

Louis Bookman played soccer for Belfast Celtic and then professionally in England for many years, winning Irish caps and also representing Ireland at cricket. Chaim Herzog, before becoming President of Israel, was Irish bantamweight boxing champion. Mark Cohen was one of Irish cricket's highest scoring batsmen and in the third millennium brothers Stephen and Greg Mollins have represented Ireland at cricket while their cousin Lara Mollins has played for the Irish Ladies cricket team.

Irish Jews have been World Junior long jump champions, international hockey umpires, driven in the Monte Carlo rally and so on. There have been Irish Jews representing Ireland at soccer, rugby, golf, cricket, athletics, chess, bridge, fencing, swimming, table tennis and wrestling. 'Oriental Way' owned by Professor Leonard Abrahamson ran, without success, in the British Grand National of 1955. Much more successful was David Vard who owned the sire of Arkle, perhaps Ireland's most famous racehorse.

Despite this full involvement in Irish sporting life, a charge of anti-Semitism can be levelled. That Jews in Belfast and Dublin formed their own golf, cricket, soccer, boxing and sailing clubs, shows signs of exclusion rather than a desire by Jews to bond together. There are many anecdotal accounts of Jews being refused admittance to the 'middle class' sporting clubs of golf and cricket. Those days may have ended, but they did exist.

Irish Jews have been prominent in literature. David Marcus is important as an author and publisher of poetry and short stories in Dublin. Beatrice Hurwitz and Harold Goldblatt were involved in the establishment of Belfast's Ulster Group Theatre, Goldblatt going on to make more than forty films. Louis Lentin had major roles in the establishment of both RTÉ and Israeli television in the 1960s. David Goldberg has alternated between a senior legal career and that of a painter. Aaron Kernoff, Harry and Gerald Davis and Estella Solomons have all been prominent artists, while Ruth Romney has been a leading sculptor.

Dr Bethel Solomons was a leading medical doctor in Dublin in the first half of the twentieth century, being Master of the Rotunda Hospital between 1926 and 1933. Dr Leonard Abrahamson, in the same generation, became Professor of Pharmacology at the Royal College of Surgeons in Ireland, Dublin, to be followed by his son Mervyn, while there have been several prominent dentists from the Jewish community. Herman Good, the son of Rev Gudansky of Adelaide Road synagogue, was one of many Jewish lawyers, becoming a judge in 1966, followed by Hubert Wine appointed in 1974 and Henry

Barron in 1982. Academics include Cornelius Lanczos, a pre-war colleague of Albert Einstein who came to Ireland in 1953 as Professor of Mathematics at the Dublin Institute for Advanced Studies, and Jacob Weingreen, Professor of Hebrew at Trinity College, Dublin from 1937 to 1978.

It is arguably in the political field that Ireland has shown its full modern acceptance of the Jewish community. Early Irish Jewish political involvement included David Ricardo, born an orthodox Jew in London, who probably converted to Christianity on marriage and who represented Portarlington at Westminster from 1819-1823. In 1876 Lewis Harris was about to take up office as Lord Mayor of Dublin when his untimely death intervened. The honour of Dublin's first Jewish Lord Mayor belongs to Robert Briscoe, serving in 1956 and 1966. Robert Briscoe was first elected Lord Mayor by his name being drawn out of a hat with the vote tied at 19 votes each. He lost the mayoral position in 1957 when his name was not drawn from the hat. Briscoe had the challenging inter-faith experience when he, an Irish Jew, represented a Catholic government in a meeting with Gandhi. Gerald Goldberg was elected Mayor of Cork in 1977 and Ben Briscoe Lord Mayor of Dublin in 1988. Robert Briscoe also served in Dáil Éireann from 1927-1965, his son Ben being elected his successor. In the 1980s and 1990s the election of Alan Shatter and Mervyn Taylor meant there were for periods three Jewish TDs representing Fianna Fáil, Fine Gael and Labour and they maintain their religion has never been an issue in the election campaigns they have fought. Chaim Herzog, President of Israel from 1983-1993, was born in Belfast in 1917 and while his subsequent military, diplomatic and political career took place outside of Ireland, he is rightly acknowledged as one of Belfast's greatest sons.

Jewish 'landmarks' in Dublin include the Irish Jewish Museum in Walworth Road, the Weingreen Biblical Antiquities Museum in Trinity College, the Holocaust Memorial in the grounds of the Rathfarnham synagogue, Stratford School in Rathgar, and the statue of Moses outside the Four Courts.

Jewish cemeteries have been preserved in Cork, in Kilmarray, Co Limerick and Limerick city, in Ballybough north Dublin, Dolphin's Barn south Dublin and Woodlawn in Rathfarnham. The Cork cemetery contains the graves of Jewish passengers from the Lusitania that was torpedoed in 1916. In 1989 Cork opened 'Shalom Park' in the area where many of the Jewish community formerly lived and Belfast's Botanic Park has a memorial fountain honouring Daniel Joseph, the father of the Jewish Lord Mayor of Belfast, Otto Jaffe.

In 2003 Ireland established a tradition of an annual Holocaust Memorial Day attended by political and civic leaders. The participation reflects the many groups, not just Jews, who were targeted in the Holocaust, but is a further example of Ireland recognising the place of her Jewish community

The interaction of the Irish Jewish community with the Christian host community may be summarised as one of increasing tolerance and acceptance. Anti-Semitic incidents are largely in the past and those that did occur were minor in comparison to events in the rest of Europe. The Irish are not as free of the charge of anti-Semitism as Daniel O'Connell liked to think with the Limerick Pogrom and the Irish government attitude to Jewish refugees in the war era as the main incidents, although as recently as February 2003 posters denying the Holocaust were distributed in Dublin universities while May 2005 saw vandalism of Jewish graves and synagogues in Dublin on the same evening. Nevertheless, when Chaim Herzog paid an official visit to Ireland in June 1985 as President of Israel, in his address at the Adelaide Road Synagogue he spoke of the Jewish community that, 'Many of them had come here from oppression. Here they found freedom and equality.'

CHAPTER FOUR

The Muslim Community in Ireland

What is Ireland's connection with the golden roof of The Dome of the Rock Mosque in Jerusalem, the third holiest Islamic centre after Mecca and Medina? In the 1990s much of the renovation of this mosque, a project of interest to world Islam, was entrusted to Mivan Construction from Northern Ireland. Northern Irish workmen replaced five thousand golden plates on the dome and placed their visible mark on a symbol of world Islam. It is worth stressing that this significant Irish-Islamic encounter was a friendly, positive and mutually beneficial experience for all involved, a good note on which to begin considering Ireland's involvement with Islam.

One of Ireland's earliest resident Muslims was Dean Mahomet, later to be known as the 'Shampooing Surgeon to King George IV'. Mahomet, originally from Patna in India, enlisted in the East India regiment aged ten and eventually reached the rank of lieutenant. He served alongside a Captain Baker and upon Baker's court martial Mahomet also resigned and both arrived in Cork in 1784. Baker married into the wealthy Massey family but died shortly after. However, the friendship was not forgotten and the Massey family appear to have assisted Mahomet's entry into Irish life. Mahomet married an Irish woman and in 1794 published *The Travels of Dean Mahomet*, probably intended as a guide for Irish involved in the British administration of India. In 1801 Mahomet moved to England and there achieved a greater level of fame. He established bath-houses in Brighton and London offering Indian massage and vapour treatments in addition to the normal bathing facilities, thus earning the title of 'shampooing surgeon'. Among his clients were

King George IV and the then Prime Minister Sir Robert Peel. Mahomet died several months after his wife in 1851 after sixty-five years of marriage and both were buried in St Nicholas' Churchyard in Brighton.

Around the same time another Muslim entrepreneur arrived in Dublin. Dr Achmet Borumborad from Turkey set himself up as the proprietor of a hot and cold sea bath establishment in Dublin, with some success. Unfortunately love did not run as smoothly for Borumborad as for Mahomet. In order to marry a Dubliner Borumborad shaved off his beard and revealed himself as the resourceful Patrick Joyce from Kilkenny. Perhaps this should remind the twenty-first century Irish that not all that purports to represent Islam truly does.

History of the Irish Muslim Community
While the substantive experience of Islam within Ireland is a relatively recent phenomenon, the interaction of the Irish with Muslims goes back to near the start of the Islamic era through the selling by Vikings of captured Irish into slavery.

Some of the earliest recorded visits of Muslims to Ireland were the raids of Moorish pirates along Ireland's southern coast in the seventeenth century. On a much smaller scale than the Viking attacks, these raids culminated in that on Baltimore in 1631 when 200 inhabitants were captured, the event commemorated in Thomas Davis' ballad *The Sack of Baltimore*. It was far from one-way traffic and the compliment was returned in the small Irish involvement in the African slave trade. The Irish registered *The Sylva* and *The Sophia* were both recorded slaving in the Gambia in May 1716 and two years later *The Prosperity* from Limerick transported ninety-six slaves from Africa to Barbados. While Irish ports did not rely on the transportation of slaves as much as British ports such as London, Liverpool and Bristol, the economies of Belfast and Dublin were bolstered by provisioning the slave dependent colonies of the Caribbean. The islands very rapidly became one crop export economies, usually tobacco, sugar or coffee, and most food for the population had to be imported. While it was not slaves moving through Irish ports, the food and supplies that filled Irish ports and ships made Ireland almost as reliant on the slave industry as Britain in the eighteenth century.

Historical records of Muslims in Ireland in the eighteenth and nineteenth centuries are sketchy although in March 1794 a theatre in Smock Alley, Dublin was destroyed by a mob after a play entitled *Mahomet* was performed. In 1791 a notable convert to Methodism in Dublin was recorded as follows:

A Turkish merchant, called Ibrahim Ben Ali, who, arriving in the city, and knowing but little English, inquired for anyone who understood either Arabic or Spanish. He was a native of Constantinople, near to which his father, a strict Mahometan, resided on a large estate. Among the many slaves he possessed were several Spaniards, who frequently spoke to Ibrahim of the God of the Christians, and of Jesus Christ, telling him that Mahomet was a false prophet and his teaching untrue. After numerous remarkable vicissitudes, at length this young man visited Ireland, and thus became acquainted with Mr Clarke, and was instructed by him more fully in the way of salvation. In the course of a few months, at his own ernest request, he was admitted to the Sacrament of baptism, which was administered in Whitefriar Street chapel by Mr Rutherford, while Mr Clarke translated the service into Spanish. This Christian Turk continued to maintain a consistent character until his death.

In less dramatic style the Roman Catholic parish baptismal register in Enniscorthy recorded the baptism of a 'convert from Mahometanism' (sic), 12 September 1853.

In the 1930s and 1940s small numbers of Indian Muslims began to settle in Northern Ireland. Some came via sugar plantations in Cuba with a Muhammad Ali coming through this route and settling near Dungannon in the mid 1920s. The dislocation to the world caused by the Second World War and the large numbers of Indians serving in Allied armies helped increase this movement, which was further supplemented in the aftermath of Indian independence and partition in 1947 when millions lost their lives. The immigrants usually arrived first in England and then moved on to Northern Ireland looking for better economic prospects.

These immigrants were generally men who only sent for their wives and children after they were settled and had achieved at least a modest level of prosperity by which they could provide for a family. Marriage to Irish women was not common but did happen. Lal Khan from what is now Pakistan 'jumped ship' in Glasgow and then came to Ireland in 1939, settling near Dungannon and working as a travelling salesman. While retaining his Muslim faith Lal married a local Catholic woman and had 12 children. After his burial, he was reburied by Muslim friends so that his body was facing Mecca, a custom not familiar to the local undertaker.

In the 1950s and 1960s further settlers arrived, often relatives of those already here and a visible Muslim population began to grow. Muslim Medical students started to study at the Royal College of Surgeons in Dublin in significant numbers.

The economic, educational and social differences between these two initial sources of Ireland's Muslim community highlights an issue common to most of the more recently established religious communities in Ireland. Often the phrase 'Muslim community' is used when it is more accurate to talk of 'communities'. The differences between Arab, Asian and African Muslims are immense, and even these regional categories imply a unity that is not justified. Additionally there is the significant Sunni-Shi'a distinction, language differences, liberal and secular interpretations, all resulting in Muslim communities rather than community. A brief glance at the variety of Christian expression found in Ireland illustrates the diversity within these other faith communities that often is overlooked.

In the early 1950s some Muslim students in Dublin were given permission by the Salvation Army to use a room for Friday prayers, although at this stage there were no resident Muslim clergy. The first Muslim organisation in Ireland was the

Dublin Islamic Society founded in 1959 by students. The first mosque in Ireland was opened in Dublin in 1975 in Harrington Street, and the first purpose built mosque in the unlikely location of Ballyhaunis in 1986, due to the presence of a Muslim meat business. In 1983 the former Donore Avenue Presbyterian Church in Dublin became the largest mosque in Ireland, to be superseded in 1996 by the opening of the impressive Islamic Cultural Centre in south Dublin. This mosque is one of the largest in Europe capable of housing over 1,000 worshippers and cost £5,000,000 to build, with significant financial assistance from the Maktoum family, rulers of Dubai. Several mosques now exist in Dublin, with further mosques in Belfast, Limerick, Cork, Galway, Ballyhaunis, Waterford and Cavan. An original burial plot in Mount Jerome Cemetery in south Dublin is now full and burials currently take place in the Muslim Graveyard in Newcastle, Co Dublin.

The Belfast Islamic Centre was formally established in 1977 and in 1986 the current mosque in Wellington Park was opened and the first resident Imam appointed in 1994. At the time of writing a controversy is running over a proposed mosque in Craigavon, which would be the first purpose built mosque in Northern Ireland. Unionist councillors have objected to the building on the grounds of noise, traffic, and pollution. Yet their objections also show a religious bias. Fred Crowe, Ulster Unionist Party councillor and a former Mayor of Craigavon, commented, 'I've been to Muslim countries around the world and I don't agree with it (Islam). I am very objective. I was elected to represent the people of Craigavon and the people don't want the mosque.' Jamal Iweida, President of the Belfast mosque, criticised the call to prayer being described as 'wailing', saying 'We respect churches and we are asking to be treated as equals.'

Sharing the Clonskeagh site is the first fully state funded Muslim National School, opened by President Mary Robinson in 1993. The school began at the South Circular Road mosque in 1990 before moving to Clonskeagh. There is a second Muslim national school in north Dublin with current plans for a Muslim secondary school. Most Irish Muslim pupils currently attend Catholic schools, generally due to their parents' preference for single sex education. While there has not been widespread difficulty there have been some situations where female Muslim pupils have been unable to wear the *hijab* as it does not conform to school uniform regulations. Jewish pupils of a previous generation usually attended Protestant schools due to the then Catholic policy of generally only admitting Catholic pupils. This change may be a sign of an increasing inter-faith tolerance. Irish boarding schools often have a number of foreign Muslim pupils.

Ireland currently has one Shi'a mosque in Milltown, south Dublin. While Shi'a Muslims are content to worship in a Sunni mosque, there is generally a desire to establish a separate place of worship when numbers justify this. In the 1970s a number of Shi'a Muslim medical students at the Royal College of Surgeons rented a house in Portabello, moving to Rathgar as numbers increased. As the community continued to grow a more stable base was desired and the present Islamic Centre was opened in 1996 with a resident Shi'a Imam. While Sunni-Shi'a differences are not recorded in the Irish census, in 2004 the Shi'a community estimated their numbers at around 1000.

WHAT IS THE IRISH MUSLIM FAITH?

The Foundation

Like many faiths, Islam does not see national or regional differences. Islam is Islam wherever it is and the title 'Irish Muslim faith' does not sit easily. Islam does not want an adjective to modify the faith. That said, there are expressions of Islam found in Ireland and so this is what is described.

Muhammad was born in Mecca some time after his father's death in AD570. Following the normal custom he was sent from his mother for the first few years of life, growing up in the desert with a Bedouin foster- mother, only being returned to his natural mother aged five. A short while later his mother died and Muhammad was raised by a grandfather and then by his uncle and 'guide' Abu Talib. The Quraysh family into which

Muhammad was born was the custodian of the existing shrine at Mecca. It was a family of influence in the community although Muhammad had few personal advantages. When he grew up he worked on the caravan train of a wealthy widow called Khadijah and aged twenty-five he married Khadijah, becoming a wealthy businessman in his own right. For the next fifteen years Muhammad traded successfully, becoming a respected businessman. He also spent time reflecting on the nature of Arab society and the unsatisfactory nature of the polytheistic worship of the people.

From around the age of thirty-five Muhammad began a practice of annual spiritual retreats, and five years later, in 610, he had an experience while meditating (or possibly while asleep) alone on a mountain which shaped the rest of his life and that of world history. An angel came to him and said, 'Read'. Muhammad replied with the reasonable comment that he was unable to read but the angel commanded him to read anyway. The words that came to Muhammad in a spiritual state are recorded in the Qu'ran and are held sacred by Muslims. They are not to be confused with words he spoke in a normal way, which are recorded in the *Sunnah of the Prophet*.

For the next three years Muhammad preached to his family, friends and the inhabitants of Mecca, the latter considering him a little mad. The first convert was his wife Khadijah, followed by his cousin Ali, then his servant Zayd. Another early convert was Abu Bakr. After three years the prophet was guided to go to Mount Safa and warn the tribe of the danger of rejecting the message of monotheism, worship of the one true God, but again Muhammad was rejected. When Muhammad started to challenge polygamy and idolatry, active persecution began with Yasir and his wife Sumayyah being counted among the first Islamic martyrs. Despite this opposition there were a few converts to this new understanding of faith, with prominent tribesman such as Hamzah and Umar ibn Al-Khattab strengthening Muhammad's position. As the Muslim community grew other inhabitants of Mecca tried to isolate them through economic boycott and ghettoised them into a small area of the city. The death of his wife and then his protector Abu Talib brought Muhammad to a very low point and a visit to the town of At-Taif brought only more rejection.

In 620, in the tenth year of his ministry, Muhammad was visited by Jibreel who led him on the back of a horse-like animal to Jerusalem. There he prayed for the souls of all who he considered to have been true prophets. He was taken into heaven where he met some of the significant prophets and was brought into the presence of Allah. It was after this experience that the five times a day regular prayer, still followed today by Ireland's devout Muslims, was introduced. These experiences (*Al Mihraj*) renewed Muhammad's faith, strengthening him in the face of renewed persecution.

In 620 Muhammad met six traders from Medina who expressed great interest in his message and the following year they returned with a number of their tribes people, resulting in the establishment of a small nucleus of believers in Medina. Muhammad already knew Medina as he had visited the city as a child, had a number of relatives there and it was the place of his father's death. After a vision Muhammad instructed his followers in Mecca to leave for Medina and a gradual migration began of the approximately one hundred and forty strong Mecca Muslim community. The Meccans became concerned that Muhammad might establish himself in Medina with the intention of launching an attack on Mecca. An assassination attempt was made on Muhammad, but he escaped with Abu Bakr and reached Medina. Later the Muslims would date the Islamic calendar from this point (622 the *Hijrah*). It marked a change for the Muslim community from being a small, despised minority led by a religious teacher, into a powerful city-state led by an inspirational political, military and religious figure. In many ways it is the most significant date in Islamic history.

In Medina the prophet laid the foundations of the Islamic State. A mosque (the Masjid an-Nabawi) was built and public prayer and preaching was instituted. Prayer had previously been offered facing Jerusalem but after sixteen months in Medina the prophet received a revelation instructing him to change direction to Mecca, a move strongly criticised by the Jewish portion of Medina. Shortly afterwards the fasting month of Ramadan was established. The Meccan immigrants mixed with the Medina believers and the economic and military might of Islam began to develop.

There followed a period of hostility between Mecca and Medina with the advantage changing several times. During a period of relative peace Muhammad attempted a pilgrimage to Mecca but was refused entry and had his messenger Uthman murdered. Despite opportunities for revenge Muhammad held back and the truce of Al-Hudaybiyah was signed allowing no hostilities for ten years; this showed a great contrast to his earlier treatment of the Jewish tribes in Medina. The Jewish tribes of northern Arabia were subdued in this period and an unsuccessful battle fought against the Persians. Muhammad had hoped the Jewish and Christian populations would accept his message but when their rejection became very plain his initial warmth to the 'People of the Book' changed to a condemnation of those who had rejected their own inheritance (*Surah* 9:30).

In 630 the Meccans broke the truce by attacking another Arab tribe that had a treaty with Muhammad. Leading an attack on Mecca, Muhammad found it relatively lightly defended and the city was captured. He entered the Kabbah shrine, cleared it of idols and established Muslim worship there.

With secure control of southwest Arabia, Muhammad's influence began to spread. Tribes came to offer tribute to avoid hostilities and through a combination of threat and attack the Muslim political and economic influence spread throughout Arabia. After a final pilgrimage to Mecca Muhammad preached to a vast crowd at Mt Arafat, calling on them to continue the spread of Islam. A brief illness followed during which Muhammad gave instructions that he was not to be worshipped or venerated, and then the prophet died in 632 in Medina, in the company of his favourite wife A'isha.

By the time of Muhammad's death, Islam had political and religious control of most of Arabia, and the next couple of generations saw rapid progress through military conquest, treaties and religious conversion.

Development of Faith

The Prophet was followed by his close friend Abu Bakr (632-34) who consolidated the inherited position and waged war on Syria and Mesopotamia. Umar (634-44) oversaw the capture of Damascus (635) and Egypt (642) and by the time of his murder the Arabs were a united empire. Uthman oversaw a period of continued political expansion, Cyprus being captured in 649 and Armenia in 652. In 653 the text of the Qu'ran was established but Uthman's corruption and the constant problem of succession led to his murder and a period of civil war between Mu'awaiya and Ali, Muhammad's cousin and son-in-law, married to his only surviving daughter Fatima. During this period an Arab navy developed and Mu'awaiya's successor Yazid defeated Ali's son, Hussein in a massacre on 10 October 680. This largely resulted in the followers of Ali and Fatima forming the Shi'ite schism in Islam.

The Umayyad Dynasty, based in Damascus, ruled from 661-750 and saw the expansion of Islam both east to Afghanistan, India and central Asia and west to Sicily (667), southern Spain (711) and Toulouse (721). This European expansion was temporarily halted by the Battle of Tours in 732.

The Abbasids (749-847) made Baghdad their capital and completed Arab unity. Arabic became the language of empire and orthodox doctrine was codified. This was a golden period with Caliphs such as Harun al Rashid of Arabian nights fame. Heading east brought contact with China in 800, moving west resulted in the capture of Palermo in 831. During the next two centuries Yemen, Corsica, Oman and the Punjab were added to the empire. In 970 the great university of Al-Azhar was established in Cairo and a naval victory won over Pisa and Genoa in 1016. But as the centre of influence shifted to Turkey the leadership became remote from the people. Arab territories such as Spain, Morocco, Algeria and Egypt began to act more as independent states and corruption set in once more.

The Seljuq dynasty (1055-1258) did not have as complete overall control as previous families and suffered constant attacks from successive Crusader armies beginning in 1096. The Mongol period from 1256-1517 saw the eastern part of the empire controlled by Mongol rulers who converted to Islam and ruled as far west as the Balkans. In the thirteenth and fourteenth centuries large parts of northern India came under Muslim control but in 1492 the last Muslim enclave in Spain, at Granada, was defeated. By this time Java, Sumatra and Sri Lanka all had considerable Muslim influence through Arab traders. In the western part of the empire the Berber tribes had great influence from the tenth to the sixteenth centuries.

The Ottoman Empire gradually developed from a small Turkish state, via the Balkans and Asia Minor, to one of the greatest Islamic empires. Constantinople was captured in 1453 and Syria and Egypt in 1516-17. Then followed Rhodes (1522), Hungary (1526), and in 1529 Vienna narrowly avoided being captured. By 1605 all of northern and central India was under Muslim control. Crete was taken in 1669.

The watershed event came in 1798-1801 with the Napoleonic invasion of Egypt. For the first time Islam was faced with a more powerful and militarily sophisticated Europe. The Ottoman Empire retreated and most of the Islamic states were colonised with the exceptions of Iran and Afghanistan. In World War I Turkey sided with Germany and Austria leading to ultimate defeat and the ending of the Caliphate in post war secular Turkey. The 1917 declaration of a homeland for Jews in Palestine and the subsequent establishment of Israel in 1948 continues to affect world history.

In this brief overview of Islamic history it is worth noting that Islam spread by the sword no more or less than Christianity. In many areas people chose to convert to Islam for religious reasons, as well as for factors related to political and economic expediency. Christian history contains similar accounts and similar excesses. Christendom is a description rarely used today as it carries connotations of violence, abuse, enslavement and coercion – none notable Christian virtues. World history tends to show that wherever a religion is dominant, that religion tends to use most available methods to maintain that position and stifle religious opposition. The recent history of Islamic Afghanistan, and contemporary Hindu India and Buddhist Burma and Sri Lanka tend to enforce this view. Catholic Ireland and Protestant Ulster, in various moments of history, have not been noted for their liberalism or pluralism. Islamic history is no better, but also no worse than this.

History does not show a united Islamic world positioned against the Christian west. There has rarely, if ever, been anything close to a united Islamic world nor does the title 'Christian west' bear much meaningful scrutiny. World War I saw a Christian-Islamic coalition comprising Germany, Austria and Turkey while western European countries, not withstanding a variety of motives, have militarily intervened to defend Islamic populations in the Balkans and Kuwait in the 1990s. The proposal to admit Turkey to the European Union is a further denial of a pan Islamic assault on the west, as is the history of conflict between Muslim majority states such as Iran-Iraq and civil wars in what was East and West Pakistan and within post-Sadam Iraq.

Beliefs

'There is no God but God and Muhammad is his prophet.' This simple phrase is all that a new convert need declare to be accepted as a follower of Islam. It is a declaration of strict monotheism and an understanding of faith as delivered through Muhammad.

Muhammad considered he was reintroducing monotheism (*tawhid*) to the world. In the passage of time since its establishment the shrine at Mecca had become polluted by numerous images to gods while the Christians had developed their trinity, although there is good evidence to consider that Muhammad thought this to be Father, Mary and Jesus. So Muhammad was calling people back to the monotheism of Abraham. The Christian claim of Jesus as God's son is unacceptable to Muslims as they see it creating a second god and implying that God had a physical sexual relationship.

The Prophet Muhammad is not considered to be a saint, seer, wonderworker or divine incarnation to Muslims; he is not a thoughtful mystic like the Buddha nor a philosopher like Confucius. Rather Muhammad was a simple spokesman for God. His life was normal and contrasts with the virgin birth of Jesus who is viewed as a sort of mystic. The miracle of Muhammad is the Qu'ran. Muhammad is the last prophet and revelation is completed through him (*Surah* 55:3-4). The life of Muhammad is to be emulated and obedience to the prophet is equivalent to obedience to God (*Surah* 4:80).

Within Islam the Qu'ran is considered the speech of God, fully dictated without any human editing. Muhammad could neither read nor write. Rather he heard the text of the Qu'ran from Jibreel (known to Christians as Gabriel), supernaturally memorised it and then passed it on to his followers. Hence Qu'ran means reading or recitation. Inspiration is considered to have been total, with the Prophet simply reciting exactly what he was given and having no active input into the words.

Over a period of twenty-three years Muhammad received portions of the Qu'ran from the angel Jibreel, passed them on to his followers who memorised and wrote down the words on palm leaves, leather or shoulder bones – it is to be presumed that a camel's shoulder bone could contain a fair amount of script! Jibreel also indicated where in the expanding corpus of scripture the latest portion should be placed. Tradition has it that every Ramadan Muhammad recited to Jibreel as much of the Qu'ran as he had received to date to check its accurate transmission, and that he recited the entire Qu'ran twice perfectly in his final year.

After Muhammad's death the task of codifying the Qu'ran fell to Abu Bakr. Zaid Ibn Thabit had been the prophet's scribe and he produced a copy of the Qu'ran, which was checked against other known versions for accuracy, known as the

Mus'haf or 'bound leaves'. This task was continued by Umar and then Uthman who passed copies to all the major Islamic cities to establish an authoritative version. All versions that deviated from this script in any way were destroyed and this process was considered completed by 646.

Muslims should only handle the Qu'ran in a state of religious purity and the physical book is treated with great respect, often being wrapped in an expensive cloth and kept in a high place to avoid accidental harm. The exact pronunciation is important and, unlike most Arabic texts, the Qu'ranic script is supplied with the short vowel-sign to ensure the greatest degree of accuracy. Readings are preceded by the phrase 'I take refuge with God from Satan, the accursed one', and followed by 'God Almighty has spoken truly'. It is a spiritual exercise to memorise the entire book, a little shorter than the New Testament.

The Qu'ran is organised into 114 *Surahs* (literally rows) or chapters, arranged approximately in order of length with the shortest at the end and the longest at the beginning, rather than chronologically or by subject. The main exception to this is the first *Surah* known as the *Fatiha* or opening, a seven verse invocation repeated during the five daily prayers. Translations of the Qu'ran into other languages are widespread but do not carry authority, which is restricted to only the Arabic text. The verse structure follows the Arabic breath pauses and does not flow as smoothly in translation. Irish mosques usually offer Arabic classes, primarily for their own members, so that followers of Islam can understand the text of the Qu'ran and the content of prayers.

Of lesser significance but still very important are the *Hadiths* or the traditions of the Prophet. Tradition as a matter of record is called *Hadith*; as a matter of obligation and to be acted on it is called *Sunna*, comprising of all that Muhammad said, did or approved. These are all in harmony with the Qu'ran and rely for verification on the Qu'ran but reinforce and flesh out its teaching. *Hadiths* are not scripture, as they did not originate with God but developed as the companions of the prophet taught their

successors all that Muhammad had said and done. Authority for
this is claimed in *Surah* 59:7, 'Whatever the Messenger gives
you, take it; and whatever he forbids you, leave it.' Sometimes
this can be taken to seemingly extreme degrees and so if the
Prophet sat to put on trousers and stood while putting on a turban some Muslims will want to emulate this behaviour. To a
meticulous degree Muhammad became the norm of true Muslim
behaviour and the unconscious source of the manners and total
conduct of the community as far as a pattern could be ascer-
tained.

The most famous of these books of *Hadiths* is called 'the
Sound Six', the oldest is the *Muwatta of Malik* and the largest is
the *Musnad of Ahmad*. The authenticity of a *Hadith* depends on
the prominence of who claimed to hear it and the succession it
was passed on through. More research is spent on proving the
authenticity of this chain than looking critically at the statement
itself. A critical tradition, while not absent in Islam, is not as pro-
nounced as in Christianity.

Differences
There are numerous differences within Islam, many of a political nature, but the major difference is that between the Sunni
majority and Shi'ite minority. Sunni Islam comprises almost
90% of world Islam, Shi'ite Islam making up most of the rest,
being found as the overwhelming majority in Iran, approximately 50% of the Iraqi population and minorities in Bahrain,
Afghanistan, Lebanon, Syria and Yemen. The Irish Muslim population appears to be close to this 90:10 ratio, although exact figures are hard to determine. Even within Shi'ite belief there are a
large number of sub groups ranging from ultra extreme to that
of the Khojas, originally from India, whose members give 10% of
their income to the Aga Khan and make pilgrimage to him.
What follows is a combination of Shi'ite beliefs rather than those
of a particular school.

Shi'ite Muslims believe that after Muhammad there was to
be a succession of Imams who were to be considered as divinely

appointed and authoritative teachers of Islam. Muhammad's successor was his cousin and son in law, Ali who waged a civil war with Mo'awiya. There had been three successors to Muhammad before Ali but Shi'a considers Ali to have been the second 'Rightly Guided Imam'. He was murdered during Ramadan by a poisoned sword. The third was Ali's son, Hussein. The next in line had been Hussein's older brother Hassan but he, perhaps seeing how history was unfolding, entered into a pact with Mo'awiya and declined his position. The succession of Rightly Guided Imam's continued through descendants of Ali and Muhammad's daughter Fatima down to the twelfth born in 869. Most of the previous eleven met unpleasant ends but the twelfth is considered to be still living but invisible, known as the 'Imam for all times', and one day will return to bring justice to the world. He is said to have disappeared as a four year old boy in a cave in Baghdad in 873. This succession is an approximation, with different Shi'ite schools understanding the lineage in slightly differing ways.

Among Shi'ites devotion is given to Hussein. He led his followers into battle when hopelessly outnumbered at Kerbela on the Euphrates, near Baghdad, Iraq in 680. All were massacred. Kerbela is now considered the centre of the Shi'a community while the shrine of Hussein at Mashhad is a popular destination for pilgrimage, rivalling the *Hajj*.

The Festival of Muharran is possibly the best-known feature of Shi'ite Islam. For the first ten days of the Islamic new year men refrain from washing or shaving and very passionate and colourful sermons are preached, reminding followers of the suffering of Hussein and his followers. On the tenth day there is a pageant re-enacting the Battle of Kerbela and part of the devotion for some is to cut themselves. In many ways within Shi'a Islam the figure of Hussein is seen as a type of suffering Christ.

Shi'a law is alive and changing, evolving through the chain of Imams who develop and interpret the Qur'an for today. There is generally a more authoritarian understanding than within Sunni Islam, the interpretation being controlled by Ayatollahs, pope-like figures with authority and a measure of infallibility.

An approximation to a trinity can be found within Shi'a faith where Muhammad is seen as bringing the revelation of Allah, Ali the interpretation and Hussein the redemption as he is considered to have sacrificed himself to reconcile Allah to humanity. Hussein, Ali and only then Muhammad is the scale of importance. The Hajj is not so significant.

Shi'a doctrine is orthodox in almost all areas with the exception of the perspective on the Imams. *Hadiths* based on Muhammad are relegated in favour of collections based on the lives and words of Ali, Hussein and their succession. The Qu'ran is interpreted in a very allegorical way that can seem at times to be only tenuously connected with the text. Some sections of Shi'ism are more intolerant than Sunni Islam, an example being that, based on *Surah* 9:28, a Shi'a Muslim may not wish to be in the company of non-Muslims.

The twelfth Imam disappeared without children, the succession ended but Shi'ites swear allegiance to this unknown or hidden Imam. Just who this Imam was is a source of debate within Shi'ism. The current Imam, as his visible representative, becomes an infallible interpreter of all things and has the right to decide issues with no real place for community consensus.

A further division within Islam is that of the Sufi. If you ever wondered where the 'Whirling Dervishes' came from, then here is your answer. Sufism is a mystical or spiritual movement within Islam that took its name from the coarse woollen garment worn by ascetics. Their main idea is not just to follow God externally in submission, but to know God intimately and eventually lose themselves in the source of his being. To help them do this Sufis generally try to live simply, although not in separated communities as Christian monks would have done. Sufism discounts intellect and reason and concentrates on the discovery of faith whereby the meaning of faith and truth is given in experimental immediacy to the seeking soul. For the last 100 years Sufism has been in decline but it was primarily in this form that Islam entered India and Indonesia and is still influential in this way in west Africa.

Worship

The call of the muezzin from the minaret is one of the characteristics of a Muslim society and community, although in Ireland
this is more likely to be a tape played on a public address system. The call goes out five times a day for *Salat* or formal prayer,
culminating at Friday noon when up to one fifth of the world's
population kneels down and prays towards Mecca. The translation of the call is:

> God is most great, God is most great. I bear witness that there
> is no God except God: I bear witness that Muhammad is the
> apostle of God.
> Come you to prayer.
> Come you to good (*falah*).
> Prayer is better than sleep. (*only at dawn prayer*)
> (Come you to the best action.) – *only in Shi'ia*
> God is most great. God is most great.
> There is no god except God.

The stated times for prayer are before sunrise, noon, mid afternoon, just before sunset and early night and this five times a
day is a compromise between the twice mentioned early in the
Qu'ran (*Surah* 20:130, 17:78) and the forty times per day prayer
that God required from Muhammad (*Surah* 11:114). The *Mihraj*
and *Hadith* established prayer five times daily and the specific
times. Within Ireland the mosques publish a daily list of prayer
times for the faithful as the seasons change.

Formal prayer is an obligation on every Muslim who is sane,
responsible and healthy. Children will often start as young as
seven and certainly by ten. During menstruation, childbirth and
nursing, women do not join in public prayer.

Prayer is not so much communication with God as an act of
submission. The Arabic words used are standard and formal, a
consequence of which is that some Irish Muslims may have limited understanding of the meaning. That is not as important as it
might first appear since prayer is primarily an act of submission
undertaken in the awareness that Allah is observing. To miss
prayer is a sin that needs to be made up later. Private prayer or

Du'a can be offered after the formal prayers are over and while this is considered good, it is an addition rather than the main aspect of the prayer time. The formal congregational prayer is considered of greater merit.

Prayer is preceded by the removal of shoes and ritual purification by water (*wudu*). Hands are washed three times up to the wrist, the mouth is rinsed three times, water is sniffed into the nose and expelled three times, the face is washed three times from forehead to chin and ear to ear, both arms are washed up to the elbows three times, then the neck and finally the feet. If water is not available, sand or even rock is acceptable. A clean surface is necessary and so prayer mats or carpets are used (*Surah* 5:6). Prayer is offered facing Mecca and is accompanied by various bows and formal movements. While a mosque is the ideal place for prayer, anywhere is acceptable, showing the believer the presence of God in the midst of his or her day. A prayer mat keeps the worshipper ceremonially clean and points to the space between the believer and the world. The prayer room in the mosque will generally be large, with a high ceiling, decorated by Arabic calligraphy of Qu'ranic verses but no representations of people or objects. There will often be a rich carpet on the floor. The plain walls are only broken by a small indentation in one wall that points the faithful to Mecca, a symbol of Islamic unity as all Muslims are pointed towards the same destination. There will also be some sort of small platform or pulpit for the Friday sermon. This preached Friday sermon is of great importance. Only believers will be present and often commentary on social or political matters is given. Music or dancing will not be part of the worship. The English word 'mosque' is a corruption of the Arabic *masjid* which means 'place of prostration.'

Prayer is led by an Imam who may be specially trained but is not a minister or priest in the Christian sense. In smaller mosques he will have a secular job and the Imam is not essential for weddings or other rituals. The worshippers stand in rows, close to each other. Touching each other, either foot to foot or shoulder to shoulder, is not a necessary part but does increase a feeling of brotherhood. It is congregational prayer as opposed to individual prayers offered together. On Friday at noon prayer is preceded by a sermon and this is the Muslim Sabbath, although it is not a day of rest as in other religions (*Surah* 62:9-10). Business will stop from approximately 12 noon-2pm and then resume. In Ireland it is mainly men who attend this service, although the Clonskeagh mosque in Dublin has a gallery for women. Men and women are generally separated in prayer for reasons of purity. If praying together in the same room, women will be in lines behind the men. Other prayers are offered on occasions such as birth, death and marriage and these prayers are often formal and ritualised. Snatches of prayer, usually Qur'anic verses, are offered spontaneously on numerous occasions such as when entering or leaving a house and starting or finishing a journey.

There is a partial understanding of the role of intercessors in prayer. Some interpretations of Islam consider that prophets, martyrs, saints and angels all can intercede but that Muhammad is truest intercessor. The belief in other intercessors is more marked in Shi'a Islam. A further tradition has it that on the final day of judgement the line of prophets from Adam to Jesus will all disclaim the privilege of intercession that passes on until it reaches Muhammad who will intercede for all the faithful.

Living the Faith

Zakat is the Muslim obligation to share wealth and is administered as a tax in most Islamic countries (*Surah* 9:11). Private wealth is partially that of the community and only valid for an individual when the generosity of *zakat* is expressed (*Surah* 2:43, 83, 110, 117, 277). Practices differ as the Qu'ran is not clear on this issue and tax has always been a contentious area in Muslim states. Pakistan introduced special *zakat* stamps to be purchased from Post Offices and ruled that general taxation could not be treated as *zakat*. Taxation is levied on the whole population, whatever their religious position, whereas *zakat* is only for Muslims. *Zakat* in Ireland can be given directly to individuals or organisations or through the mosque.

Zakat is usually a 'tax' of 2½ % on a person's capital and is given to help the poor, widows, orphans and needy within the Muslim community and to promote missionary work. It is not regarded as a charity but as an act of purification and a way to distribute wealth to the poor (*Surah* 9:34-35, see also 3:180). Additional alms giving are required such as one day's food for a feast at the end of Ramadan. Further acts of generosity that are voluntary are known as *sadaqat* and can be directed towards needy non-Muslims.

Ramadan is a 28-day month (9th month) where Muslims fast from dawn until dusk. As the Muslim year follows a 355 day lunar calendar, this period gradually moves throughout the seasons (*Surah* 9:37). It appears to have been an Arab tradition before Islam (*Surah* 2:183) and today is arguably more popular than daily prayer. It commemorates the time of the revelation of the first of the Qu'ran and also the first military victory at Badr in 624. During this month Muslims will abstain from eating or drinking during the daylight hours, times that are defined when a black thread can be distinguished from a white thread (*Surah* 2:187). The month is to be spent in prayer, attendance at Mosque and studying the Qu'ran while each evening family and friends join for a meal with traditional dishes. This Ramadan meal can be used as an opportunity to invite non-Muslims and hence be an evangelistic opportunity. Ramadan causes a considerable amount of hardship in hot countries and the business life of Islamic countries is considerably affected, but as in most things Islamic it is a test of your submission to Allah and not to be modified. The Irish climate limits the impact of some aspects of Ramadan for Irish Muslims, although when the month occurs during an Irish summer the very long hours of daylight are a challenge. Ramadan in an Irish winter may be much more enjoyable. In some ways Ramadan can be compared to the Christian period of Lent. Asceticism on its own is considered of no benefit; rather the spiritual dimension is emphasised. Within Ireland the dates and exact times for prayer and daylight are published by the mosques with regional differences due to slightly differing sunrise and sunset times across Ireland. The fast ends with the celebration of *'id al-fitr* when visits and gifts are exchanged and special alms given in a spirit of thanksgiving. This has some similarities to the Christian festival of Christmas.

The high point of a Muslim's life is to go on *Hajj* or pilgrimage. At least once in a believer's life he or she is called to make the *Hajj* unless finance or illness prevents (*Surah* 3:97). Those that succeed are honoured in the Muslim community and carry the title of Al Haj with their name. Irish Muslims are enthusiastic participants and in 2005 ninety-seven comprised the organised Irish group. The pilgrimage is made during Dhu'lhijah (the last month) but can be taken at other times (*Surah* 2:196, 3:97). No 'observers' are allowed and non-Muslims are forbidden to enter Mecca. Mecca is the destination for a variety of reasons. It is where creation is considered to have begun; Abraham called by God to journey to Mecca; when Ismail was thirsty his heel struck the ground and a spring of water came out at Mecca, and Abraham restored the shrine at Mecca built by Adam around the Kaaba stone. It is believed that Gabriel brought this stone from heaven and the offer of Ishmail in sacrifice was at Mecca – the Dome of Rock Mosque in Jerusalem also commemorates this.

Until the discovery of oil in the 1930s much of Arabia's income came from *Hajj* pilgrims. At Mecca they find a circular Mosque with no direction they must face. Instead of pointing towards Mecca they have arrived at the place one fifth of the world looks towards. Inside the mosque is the Kaaba stone contained in a small building. The room is believed to be a replica of heaven and here believers consider themselves to be closer to heaven than at any other point on earth. Planes are forbidden to fly over Mecca and tradition has it that birds do not fly directly over the stone.

Pilgrims approaching the city stop, ritually cleanse themselves and change into plain white garments to show equality. Women are to be unveiled but often choose to wear a veil that does not touch the skin. Upon entering the Kaaba they kiss or

touch the building then circle seven times barefoot, before running between two small hills (Safa and Marwa – four hundred
and fifty yards apart) seven times to remember Hagar running
about looking for water. The pilgrims then go to the tented city
at Mina where all stay, a further mark of equality. They travel to
Mt Aarafat and stand there from noon to dusk symbolising the
last judgement and recalling Muhammad's last sermon. Arafat
is also the place where Adam and Eve were separated after the
fall and then reunited. The pilgrims return to Mina where they
throw stones at three jars representing the three times Satan
tempted Abraham over the offered sacrifice of Ishmail. On the
final day of the month a goat is sacrificed and the meat given to
the poor at the 'Feast of Sacrifice'. This part is celebrated by
Muslims worldwide and not just those on the *Hajj*. Upon return
to Mecca pilgrims cut their hair, circle the Kaaba once more and
the *Hajj* is completed. Some choose to travel on to Medina and
visit Muhammad's mosque and tomb but that is not a necessary
part of the *Hajj*.

Islam has no secular/sacred divide and so for Muslims law
needs to be Islamic law. For a Muslim to live under Shari'a Law
is an attempt to live out your faith and show complete submission to God in all things. In some ways it mirrors the approach
under the English Commonwealth of Oliver Cromwell or John
Calvin's Geneva. This approach causes problems when a Muslim
majority introduce Shari'a law in a state that has a significant
non-Muslim population. Contemporary examples include Sudan
and Nigeria. Yet part of the Muslim response is that Shari'a is
God's way and while it is obligatory for Muslims it is also the
best way for all to live because it is God's way. In the 1950s
Ireland had something close to two Christian law codes in
Protestant Northern Ireland and Roman Catholic Republic of
Ireland. Not quite Irish Christian versions of Shar'ia, but a comparison is valid.

This law, rather than theology, has the prior emphasis in
Islam. Broadly, it is obedience to the will of God rather than fellowship in the awareness of God's love. It is considered that it is

possible for an individual to follow this law and so show true submission. The true form of the family, state and economy are discovered in the divine will expressed in the Shari'a. No other appeals to human rights or women's rights are of equal relevance because God has revealed the blueprint and the Muslim has to submit and follow.

Shari'a Law is the Qur'an expanded by recognised jurists, the *muftis/mullahs* who depend on *hadiths*. It is not codified or uniform in the sense of western law but has been developed and elaborated over the centuries. Arguably it has never been properly tried; it would seem that it could only work properly in a fully Islamic faith society. This law is applied to cases through the use of *qiyas*, scholarly interpretation often by analogy / precedent or *ijma*, community consensus. Muhammad said, 'My people will never be unanimous in error.'

Ijma can lead to development and change in Shari'a although is generally only used when other roots are not clear. It is tempered by restricting community consensus to a few wise men rather than the full community. At an extreme this means that Islam is what Muslims define it to be. *Ijtihad* is the process whereby *ijma* is achieved. Qualified *mujtahids* or scholars discuss and arrive at conclusions for the people. This deals with the law and not dogma but allows Islamic countries to change laws by a parliamentary type system and claim it as Islamic as it is an expression of the popular will or *ijma*. The *Sunna* (the way) or legal code, binding all Muslims, is the result.

Following this law demands complete submission and the law is as concerned with enforcing what is thought as good as it is in stopping what is considered evil (*Surah* 3:104, 110). Based on the Qur'an and the *Hadiths*, the words and example of Muhammad are very significant. Even Muhammad's silence on a subject is considered significant, implying he did not oppose an act or custom practised by early Muslims. Law can be considered in five categories:

1. what God has commanded
2. what God has recommended but not made compulsory

3. what God has left neutral

4. what God does not encourage but has not prohibited

5. what God has clearly forbidden

In Muslim countries during the latter part of the nineteenth century and the early years of the twentieth century existing versions of Shari'a Law were weakened and secular laws were introduced based on western law codes. However, the rise of a more Islamist approach coupled with the emerging economic strength of Muslim countries has led a number of Muslim nations to reintroduce Shari'a either in part or whole. This is part of a debate within Islam as Shar'ia challenges practices that are common in many conservative Muslim countries, such as hereditary government and the payment of interest.

What is Islamic Fundamentalism?

The term 'fundamentalist' was first used in a religious context in the early years of the twentieth century to identify Christians who believed and actively defended a conservative and literalist Protestant Christian belief. A series of booklets called 'The Fundamentals' were published between 1910-15 that opposed those who were accepting the fruits of liberal scholarship and scientific interpretations such as Darwinism. These conservative Protestants used proactive approaches such as publishing articles and organising rallies to raise public awareness of what was happening. Their beliefs were largely that:

1. they have the true understanding of the faith

2. scripture was to be interpreted literally

3. history was a battle between God and Satan, and they were now fighting for God

4. traditions were to be upheld, not changed

5. political action was part of the faith

6. their view of morality was to be enforced on all (society viewed as in moral decay)

7. their understanding of faith should be the only view taught

8. those that differed were at best deluded and at worst on the side of Satan

In Ireland this approach is most readily seen in the work of Revd Ian Paisley and the Free Presbyterian Church. An important aspect of fundamentalism is the stress on the prominence of religious values and beliefs in social and political contexts and so the religious leader can also become the political leader, or at least the main influence on the politician.

Given this particular Christian usage it is not appropriate to apply the term to Islam. It is more accurate to use Islamist rather than fundamentalist. Many Muslims rightly feel that Islam is being caricatured and that a small extreme minority is being considered as representative of all that is Islam. Within Ireland what also needs to be recognised is that many Muslims came here because they perceived that in Ireland they would be free from the clerical domination that characterises some Islamic societies. Many are economic migrants attracted to life in a secular nation. Ireland has had earlier experiences of foreign religious communities coming here to escape religious persecution, the Huguenots being a notable example. Ireland's Muslim communities are not a parallel with the Huguenot experience, but the point is still valid. To look on Ireland's Muslim communities and equate them with the extreme images our news coverage often portrays is to do a great disservice to both truth and Ireland's Muslims.

Islam believes that faith cannot be forced (*Surah* 2:256) and that respect must be given in particular to Christians and Jews as 'People of the Book' who worship the same God (*Surah* 29:46). Tolerance among nations was key (*Surah* 49:13) and so medieval Spain under Muslim rule was a refuge for religious dissidents. In Moghul or Muslim ruled India the experience of the majority Hindu population was generally, although not always, one of religious tolerance and pluralism in society. What is sometimes inaccurately described today as Islamic fundamentalism is not the heart of Islam but a distortion of the faith.

Modern Islamism grew in the aftermath of the 1967 war when the Arab nations were defeated by Israel. Before that some Arab countries had tried to escape western dominance by imitating western institutions. However 1967 resulted in an alternative

approach prevailing, to return to Islamic cultural values and institutions and to reject western influence. Among the countries
changed dramatically were Iran where the pro-western government was overthrown in 1979, and Afghanistan where the
Russian dominated government was defeated in a conflict cross-
ing the 1980s and 1990s. As recent history shows, not all these
changes are permanent.

Islam has been caricatured as a warlike religion. The reality is
that pre-Islamic Arabia was caught up in a vicious cycle of warfare
in which tribes fought each other in vendettas. After having to
fight for the survival of the early Muslim community, Muhammad
brought peace through alliances to Arabia. Many passages of the
Qu'ran deal with warfare and can be quoted selectively by those
advocating violence, an approach not unknown in Christianity.
Thus *Surah* 4:89 says that Muslims are ordered to 'slay (enemies)
wherever you find them.' But a continuation into *Surah* 4:90 de-
clares 'Thus, if they let you be, and do not make war on you, and
offer you peace, God does not allow you to harm them.'

Jihad is not one of the five pillars or essentials of Islam. It
means struggle and the greater *jihad* is the inward struggle to
overcome sin and submit to God. The lesser *jihad* is the physical
battle to impose God's rule on society. In the Qu'ran the only
permissible war is one of self-defence. Muslims may not begin
hostilities (*Surah* 2:190). Warfare is always evil but sometimes
you have to fight to avoid the kind of persecution that Mecca in-
flicted on the early Muslim community (*Surah* 2:191, 2:217) or to
preserve decent values (*Surah* 4:75, 22:40). It is considered good
to forgo revenge in a spirit of charity (*Surah* 5:45) and hostilities
must be as short as possible and stop as soon as the enemy
wants peace (*Surah* 2:192-3).

Almost every religion has aspects of violence in its foundation and early history; some contain aspects of terrorism and
genocide or its modern term 'ethnic cleansing'. The Judeo/
Christian history has more than its fair share of such history as
does Islam, but it is important to note that Islam is not unique in
a connection to violence.

The early history of the Islamic community is of a small pow-
erless people being persecuted in Mecca and eventually moving
to Medina for survival. Due to spiritual growth and political alliances the community became stronger and eventually military
campaigns and what we might today call terrorism were enacted.
The subsequent history is one of conquest and defeat, much as
any empire and it cannot be argued that Islam is unique in having a partially violent beginning. Where it may differ from
Christianity is in a development from an Old Testament to a
New Testament understanding. To some extent Islam remains
rooted in its sixth century origins and a generally literalist understanding of scripture does not encourage much development. When compared to Jesus, Muhammad is a much more
worldly, politically and militarily involved character. Although
Christianity does have its own recent history of the apartheid
regime in South Africa receiving, for a time, theological justification from a section of the Dutch Reformed Church, and Ulster
history shows aspects of legitimation claimed by terrorists of
different Christian backgrounds.

However, with all the above qualifications, there remains a
justification for violence under certain specific conditions within
Islam that gives a theological underpinning to extremists that
Christian background terrorists cannot have.

Adaptation and Contribution to Ireland

Like the other smaller Irish religious communities, Muslims
have suffered in the Northern Ireland conflict. On 26 June 1973
Noorbaz Khan, originally from Pakistan and working as a civil-
ian lorry driver for the British army, was murdered by the IRA
in Londonderry. Less than a year later, on 22 April 1974
Mohammed Khalid, who provided British soldiers with tea and
other refreshments, was murdered by the IRA in Crossmaglen,
Co Armagh.

Muslim marriage practice, whereby a man can have up to
four wives, runs contrary to Irish and British law. While the
Qur'an appears to allow for up to four wives (*Surah* 4:3) this

verse can be considered as disapproving of more than one wife as there is a command to treat all equally and this is virtually impossible to do. Muhammad had more than four wives, perhaps up to eleven, although he remained married only to Khadijah, his first wife, during her life. This issue highlights the difficulties for newcomers who wish to hold on to their cultural and religious practices but find they conflict with the laws of their new land. Britain and Ireland have shown willingness at times to adapt laws to assist new religious communities – halal meat practices and Sikhs being allowed to wear turbans on motorbikes are but two examples. However it is unlikely that marriage laws will change in the near future.

Like Ireland's Jews, Muslims have made their mark politically, although not to the same extent. The first Irish Muslim TD was Moosaje Bhamjee elected in 1992. A medical doctor and member of the Labour party, Bhamjee represented Clare for one term. Coming from South Africa to study at the Royal College of Surgeons from 1965 to 1971, it was in Dublin that Bhamjee met his future wife, Claire. Returning to South Africa on graduation was difficult for the couple as the then government's apartheid laws made their relationship basically illegal. They returned to Ireland in 1975 and married with Muslim and Catholic ceremonies and eventually Bhamjee established himself as a psychiatrist in Ennis. After his brief spell in the Dáil Bhamjee settled back to his medical work and position as a leading citizen of the west of Ireland. He may have been an unusual coach of the Ballyrea Under Sixteen's girls' Gaelic football team, but this colourful character has provided an early role model of adaptation and integration into Irish life.

Ireland's Muslim community has its own newspaper, the *Friday Times*. Established in 2003 and published every fortnight, the paper seeks to keep Ireland's Muslims informed of items of interest both locally and internationally and be in some sense an introduction to Ireland's Muslims for the wider community. A further attempt to make Islam relevant to the wider Irish population has been the translation of the Qu'ran into Irish in 2003.

While never intended to be a mass-market initiative and aided by clauses in the Good Friday Agreement of 1997, it is one more example of Islam inculturating itself in Irish life. It is not thought that an Ulster-Scots translation will be soon forthcoming.

As Ireland's largest non-Christian religious community, Muslims are an increasingly visible part of the Irish religious and geographical landscape. While their significant history is very recent it is to be expected and welcomed that Muslims in Ireland will increasingly make their mark on Irish society and contribute towards what it means to be Irish.

CHAPTER FIVE

Hindus in Ireland

Irish people are influenced by Hinduism to an extent not generally recognised. Whether it is through vaguely 'New Age' ideas, practicing yoga, being vegetarian or following the more adventurous suggestions of the *Karma Sutra*, aspects of Hinduism impact most Irish people, beyond the Irish who practice this faith. Reference has been made earlier of the visits to Ireland of leading Indian politicians and the significant Irish involvement in India where Hinduism, as the predominate religion – or more accurately religions – was the ever present backdrop.

Where would you expect to find a Nobel Peace Prize winner queuing on his knees to be hugged by a Hindu saint? Well, the answer is contemporary Dublin where John Hume found himself part of a large crowd patiently waiting their turn. Mata Amritanandamayi Devi, known as Amma the 'Hugging Saint', sat for two days in the Royal Dublin Society Hall in November 2004 offering hugs to an estimated crowd of up to 10,000. Originally from Kerala, India Amma is considered a saint by many and is reputed to have hugged over thirty million people, to release the 'divine motherhood' within all.

Ireland has had its resident Hindu celebrities. In the 1920s one of the top international cricketers of the day, an Indian prince, bought Ballynahinch Castle in Connemara. His Highness Shri Sir Ranjitsinhji Vibhaji, Maharajah Jam Saheb of Nawanagar, spent his summers in Ireland from 1924 to 1932 accompanied by an entourage of servants and associates as befitted an Indian prince in the final days of the Raj. During his college days Ranji, although a Hindu, had been placed in the care of Revd Louis Borissow, an Anglican Chaplain of Cambridge University.

Ranji, in a similar way to many anglicised Indians, adopted western dress, food and travel habits, much of which went against a strict interpretation of Hinduism. Just travelling across the ocean broke caste obligations under a conservative understanding of the faith. In both Ireland and England Ranji illustrated a pluralist outlook traditional to Hinduism and befriended Anglican and Catholic clergy, supporting causes in both churches. In Connemara a close friendship developed with Fr White, transport was laid on so that the estate workers were able to attend Mass, and the picture is one of a benevolent landlord taking an interest in the spiritual life of his adopted country. White's successor, Fr Cunningham, was very much opposed to Ranji's presence, probably more due to racist than religious attitudes. Two of Ranji's nieces were educated at Kylemore Abbey, Connemara, staffed by Irish Benedictine nuns in the 1920s, and they seemed to have been more orthodox Hindus than their uncle, following Hindu food codes and being exempt from attending Christian services. From Ranji's stay in Ireland a picture emerges of a generally tolerant society that accepted an unusual figure and allowed him and his entourage to participate fully in community life, although with occasional discordant voices.

Ireland also has experience of a 'bogus' maharajah. In Drumcondra Churchyard, Dublin there is a headstone dated 1956 and inscribed in memory of the 'Rajah of Frongoch'. Jimmy Mulkerns had been imprisoned in Frongoch, Wales after the 1916 Rising and apparently he often amused his fellow internees by dressing up as a rajah.

History of Ireland's Hindu Community
In the 1930s and 1940s small numbers of Indians started to settle in Ireland. The dislocation to the world caused by the Second World War and the large numbers of Indians serving in Allied armies helped increase this movement. There was a further impetus to migrate in the aftermath of Indian independence and partition in 1947 when there was large loss of life and forced migration for millions who found themselves on the 'wrong'

side of a newly drawn line on the map. Many of the initial influx
of Hindus were from Lahore in Pakistan from where 300,000
Hindus and Sikhs fled after partition.

These first settlers had few qualifications and were generally
economically poor, although at the same time a steady stream of
subcontinent students and medical personnel was beginning,
most of these coming from wealthy backgrounds. The immigrants
usually arrived first in England with a few moving on to Northern
Ireland looking for better economic prospects, often setting themselves up as travelling salesmen in a similar way to many of the
Jewish immigrants from Lithuania at the end of the nineteenth
century. These early Hindu immigrants were generally single men
who only sent for their wives and children after they were settled
and had achieved at least a modest level of prosperity by which
they could provide for a family. Given the tradition of arranged
marriage, many of these young male settlers sent back word to
their families of their increasing economic circumstances and that
they were interested in becoming married. A most suitable bride
was usually forthcoming for these eligible bachelors. Marriage to
Irish women was not common but did happen.

An India League was established in Dublin to meet the cultural interests of the Indian community in the city. Many of these
came to Ireland a different route, having been settled in South
Africa for several generations before travelling to Ireland. The
Irish Anti-Apartheid movement partially grew out of this
group. A similar group was formed in Belfast in 1959.

In the early 1950s there was no resident Hindu clergy or temple in Ireland. This was not so much of a problem to the Hindu
community whose strong traditions of household shrines and
worship were family orientated, but the community had to
arrange for clergy to come from England or Scotland for the various 'rites of passage'. In 1980 Dr J. P. Singh, the then High
Commissioner of India, opened the former Carlisle Memorial
Methodist Church hall in Belfast as the Indian Community
Centre, containing a Hindu Temple, K. D. Shastri becoming the
first resident priest in 1985.

In 2003 members of Dublin's Hindu community established a committee to look at the possibility of opening a Temple. An initial worship ceremony devoted to the gods Vinayaka, Saraswathi and Lakshmi was attended by approximately 225 people and monthly worship events are now held.

Differences
Hindu differences are hard to encapsulate as there is no orthodox Hindu expression from which other views deviate. That said, there are three main types of Hindu expression:
1. Village Hinduism based on local beliefs and customs practiced by approximately 75% of Hindus.
2. Vedic Hinduism practiced by priests, scholars and ascetics, amounting to perhaps 15% of the Hindu population.
3. Renaissance Hinduism followed by the urban middle class and based on gurus and missions with perhaps 10% of Hindus following this expression of faith. Many Irish Hindus will follow this general expression.

A distinctive Hindu expression is that of ISKCON – the International Society for Krishna Consciousness, better known as Hare Krishna, that has moved from being considered by some to be a cult in the 1960s and 1970s to being accepted as a variant, although acceptable, form of Hinduism. There is a small Hare Krishna community in Ireland. A temple was opened in Dunmurry, Belfast in 1979 and a community live on Innis Rath island in Co Fermanagh. There is currently no temple in Dublin but a small community is associated with Govindas vegetarian restaurant in Aungier St. A small temple was established in Cork in 2002. A Hare Krishna community in Co Wicklow has included a convicted former IRA member among its members.

ISKCON's origins can be traced to fifteenth century Bengal and the reformer Chaitanya who was a devotee of Krishna, and who travelled widely in north India encouraging devotion to Krishna through the chanting of simple mantras. The movement remained very small until 1933 and the initiation of Prabhupada into the Gaudiya Vaisnava Mission. In 1966 he initiated his first disciples and began the practices for which they are well known today. Large numbers were attracted during the 1970s and early 1980s but there are relatively few new converts today. While western society as a whole may not be impacted by ISKCON as much as once thought, the Hindu communities in western nations, including Ireland, have welcomed much of the movement.

ISKCON belongs to the Gaudiya Vaisnava tradition, a devotional movement based on the teachings of *Bhagavad-Gita* and *Srimad-Bhagavatam* and as such is part of Hinduism and can be seen as a missionary organisation within Hinduism. It is famous for the saffron-robed devotees chanting the mantra: *Hare Krishna Hare Krishna, Krishna Krishna, Hare Hare, Hare Rama, Hare Rama, Rama Rama, Hare Hare.* (Krishna literally means the most beautiful of all and Rama the reservoir of all pleasure). Essentials of ISKCON that do not make it obviously attractive to the Irish population include a prohibition on alcohol, gambling and sexual intercourse for any other reason than conceiving a child. These views, alongside dietary and clothing restrictions, also place the movement beyond the very loose boundaries of mainstream Hinduism.

Is ISKCON a cult? This question was asked by a previous generation of Irish more so than today and often operates on the level of interpretation rather than fact. Certainly ISKCON has been accused of being a cult in the past but many of the characteristics pointed to could well be alluded to in many more mainstream religious groups. There have been well-documented incidents worldwide of the use of 'brainwashing' techniques, undue control over members' finances, a patriarchal structure, the sexual exploitation of women and children, religious teachers living extravagant lifestyles and the use of drugs, all in the past. Much of the above can also be said about members of both mainstream religions and variant groups within particular faith communities. A deeper consideration reveals than none of the above activities are essential components of ISKCON. In twenty-first century Ireland ISKCON is a variation of traditional Hindu belief and part of a maturing worldwide missionary movement.

The contemporary Irish Hare Krishna community operates

much like a Christian congregation. Members live in the wider population with only a very small number forming a resident community. Devotees take 'normal' employment and marry. Attendance at worship is akin to Christians attending church services. In Northern Ireland the Hare Krishna community has actively participated in the Northern Ireland Inter-Faith Forum since its inception in 1993 with a member serving on its Executive Committee. There is an increasing interaction with the wider Hindu community through participation in events at the Hare Krishna temple.

Of lesser impact in Ireland has been the Transcendental Meditation (TM) of Guru Maharishi Mahesh Yogi who had an influence on George Harrison and other members of 'The Beatles'. TM is based on the Vedas and some argue that it can be used as a meditation technique independent of Hinduism. The Natural Law Party, based on this teaching, has attracted a few dozen votes in British parliamentary constituencies, including Northern Ireland, in the last few British general elections.

Yoga, literally meaning the act of yoking another, is often billed as a keep fit and relaxation technique but that is only part of the story as yoga attempts to empty the mind and then let it be filled with our inner goodness. Many Irish community halls have yoga classes and while most participate for exercise, the Hindu roots of yoga should never be discounted.

WHAT IS THE IRISH HINDU FAITH?

Foundation
In the eighteenth century the British coined the word 'Hinduism' to describe the religious life of the people of India. Arguably Hinduism is an artificial construct that seeks to join to-gether various related but independent religious traditions. It is helpful to think of Hinduism as a network of related religions rather than one monolithic faith.

The History of Hinduism

The initial Irish Hindu link is lost in the myths of time as the Aryan race of European origin, that spread as far west as Ireland and as far east as Iran and India, entering India around 1700BC. From the Veda scriptures we gain most of our knowledge of these people and principally from the *Rig-Veda*, which was composed by the priests who were responsible for the fire sacrifices. The gods worshipped were mostly male and often concerned with natural phenomena such as storms and rain. Links, although far from conclusive, can be drawn between some basic Hindu concepts and aspects of Celtic religion.

These Aryans brought an embryonic caste system, of either two or three tiers. They believed in a cosmic principal, *Rta*, that was precarious and had to be sustained by sacrifice as well as the proper performance of *dharma*. In this early society priests rose to prominence, guided by the *shastras* or manuals concerning the conduct of rituals and the ordering of society. The transmigration or reincarnation of souls was not prominent in Vedic teaching.

When the Aryans arrived in what is now the Indian subcontinent they found dark skinned inhabitants whom they conquered and then intermarried with. The primal religion of this Dravidian community seems to have concentrated on fertility cults, with images of the mother goddess and the phallus. Archaeological finds suggest a system of temple worship with ritual washing or purification. It is now common to suggest that these two forms of religion blended and produced early Hinduism that emerged around 200BC. However, in a country as vast as India few simple explanations work. What is clear is that beliefs such as rebirth, *samsara* and *karma* are very rarely found in the Vedas, yet became prominent in Hinduism.

A major figure in the development of Hinduism was Sankara (AD788-820). He produced commentaries on the *Upanishads*, founded four still existing monasteries and debated with Buddhists and Jains, winning back to Hinduism many who had been attracted to these other faiths. Hinduism had a series of reformers in the tenth to the fifteenth centuries including Ramanuja, Vallabha and Caitanya. To differing degrees they promoted devotion within Hinduism, encouraged a form of monotheism and attempted to mitigate the excesses of caste by their own examples.

Islam first encountered Hinduism through Arab traders but it was not until 1001 that Islam made a major impact through the raids of Mahmud of Ghazni who occupied the Punjab. A succession of invasions meant that by 1526 northern India was under Muslim Mughal rule. This rule was generally tolerant, rulers intermarried with Hindu princesses and Hindu practices were allowed at court. While taxes were imposed on non-Muslim subjects, often Brahmins were excluded and temples received government grants. Yet there were exceptions such as Aurangzeb (1658-1701) who demolished temples, built mosques on their sites and closed Hindu schools. This policy eventually led to the decline of Mughal rule as these intolerant practices prompted localised rebellions.

On 20 May 1498 Vasco de Gama sailed into Calcutta and opened up India to western influence. In 1757 the British defeated the French in a campaign in which we have previously noted the significant Irish involvement on both sides, and so replaced the Mughal Empire as rulers of India until 1947. The British colonialists initially opposed the introduction of missionaries to avoid alienating the Hindu population. Later generations, inspired by the ideals of the Clapham Sect and other leading English evangelicals, opposed various aspects of Hinduism such as caste, child brides and the treatment of widows that appeared primitive to a liberal, enlightened European mind. Those same generations were usually not so horrified at British excesses in India.

As a living faith Hinduism has continued to develop and prominent individuals or movements within Hinduism of recent times include Ram Mohan Roy (1772-1833) who opposed the practice of *sati* (the burning of widows) and child marriages. He was influenced by Sufism and considered some aspects of Hinduism to be idol worship. Whether Christianity influenced

Roy is questionable but his 'reformation' of Hinduism made the faith more attractive to the growing numbers of educated Indians who were being attracted to Christianity. He travelled widely in Britain and Europe. The Brahma Samaj was founded by Roy in 1830 and met on Sunday evenings to worship in a monotheistic way. Its membership was usually high caste and intellectual. After Roy's death, Muslim and Christian elements were incorporated into the movement but the rising tide of nationalism in the twentieth century led to the movement becoming marginalised.

The Arya Samaj of Dayananda Saraswati was dedicated to the restoration of pure Vedic religion. Saraswati was born in Gujarat in 1824 and turned against the worship of idols. He attempted to live the life of a *sadhu* or wandering religious ascetic and to reform Hinduism of image worship, caste and extreme aspects of village faith. He considered the Vedas to be the oldest and purest scriptures of humanity teaching one complete, eternal, holy and just God, consequently dealings between people should be based on love and justice. The movement was strongly nationalistic and suspicious of western influence.

Sri Ramakrishna (1834-1886) believed God could be found in all religions and preached a traditional Hindu tolerance. He was prepared to adapt to the dress, food and prayer patterns of whatever group he was with, had a great influence among the westernised educated Indians and led to a return to Hinduism for many who had become attracted to Christianity. He developed a series of Ashrams or open retreat houses. His main disciple was Vivekananda who attended the World's Parliament of Religions in Chicago in 1893 and revealed the riches of Hinduism to a western audience. A fiery speaker, Ramakrishna motivated Indians to have a greater concern for the needy in their own society. Both accepted caste as part of the natural order.

Bhimrao Ranji Ambedkar (1891-1956) was from the untouchable caste. Educated abroad with an American doctorate, upon returning to India in 1917 he discovered his education counted for nothing when compared to his low caste. Ambedkar became champion of untouchable rights and opposition to caste, was Law minister in post-independence India and eventually converted to Buddhism with 600,000 followers over the issue of caste.

Gandhi (1869-1948) had been influenced by Vivekananda and saw truth as God and non-violence as the path to meeting God. His liberal understanding of Hinduism encompassed all that was good from other religions. Caste was rejected and a particular concern expressed for the untouchable groups, wanting them seen as *Harijan* or 'Children of God'. In his ashrams Gandhi demanded the pursuit of truth, non-violence, abstinence from sexual activity and poverty. He was a devotee of Rama.

Satya Sai Baba (1926-present) has declared himself the incarnation of Sai Baba of Shirdi and teaches that God is beyond form and that appearance is illusion. Love and God are one and so worship consists of devotional songs, many miracles are claimed and values of truth, tolerance and non-violence respected.

There are conservative versions of Hinduism, notably embodied in the Bharatiya Janata Party of India that couples nationalism with a questioning of the traditionally tolerant pluralist nature of Hinduism.

Beliefs

Scripture does not play a central role in Hinduism in the way that it does in Islam, Sikhism or Christianity. Even within a temple copies of texts might be hard to find. More likely words of scripture will have been memorised by the priest and worshippers and used from memory in acts of devotion. The earliest Hindu scriptures are believed to have been composed between 1200BC and 1000BC by the Aryan invaders who settled in northwest India around 1500BC. A prolific creation of scripture occurred between 1200BC and 200BC, known as the Vedic Age. These Vedas are believed to have been received as revelation from God and passed on by word of mouth, known as *Shruti* or hearing as they were heard by scholars and are considered as eternal. Today scholars will still often prefer to recite a text from memory rather than use a printed copy. The main exception to this will be when thanksgiving *pura* is performed and, while mantras are recited from memory, the priest will read the story of the origin of the ritual. Two further exceptions are Krishna's birthday and during the Ganesha festival when listening to scripture being read is considered an act of devotion.

There are four Vedas, each composed of four separate parts:

1. *Rig-Veda Samhita* is the oldest and is divided into ten books or mandalas and includes 1028 hymns of praise to ancient gods. Various aspects of deity are described and the ultimate answer to life is that Brahman is the one who encompasses all.

2. *Yajur-Veda Samhita* was used as a handbook for priests performing Vedic sacrifices.

3. *Sama-Veda Samhita* consists of chants, melodies and tunes to be sung at special sacrifices.

4. *Atharva-Veda Samhita* preserves many pre-Aryan traditions concerning spells, charms and magic formulae.

Many mantras from these texts are used in modern Hindu worship such as the *Gayatri* verse from the *Rig-Veda*, often used in daily worship.

Hindu scripture is not limited to these four texts. The *Brahmanas* (800-500BC) are prose manuals of ritual and prayer for the guidance of priests. The *Aranyakas* (400-200BC) resulted from discussions in the forests about worship, meditation and ritual. The *Upanishads* (400-200BC) contain mystical concepts of Hindu philosophy, the word meaning 'near sitting' implying that they were delivered as a discourse from a guru to a pupil. In the development of scripture the physical sacrifices of the Vedas are replaced by internal attitudes. Among the important doctrinal ideas to come from these texts are:

1. the individual soul (*atman*) and the universal soul (*Brahman*) are identical

2. *Brahman* is without form and eternal

3. The visible world is an illusion (*maya*)

4. The soul passes through a cycle of successive lives (*sam-sara*) and its next existence is determined by the consequences of its actions (*karma*) in the previous existence.

5. The soul is capable of achieving liberation (*moksha*)

6. There is a unity of all things in the created universe

The popular Hindu epics, the *Mahabharata* and the *Ramayana*, are classed as *smriti* texts and include religious, moral and educational writings based on remembered tradition. Composed from 500BC onwards most Hindus accept the teachings of these in as much as they do not contradict the *shruti* texts that are considered to be more directly God's word.

The *Ramayana* or 'Adventure of Rama' is the story of a Prince from north India who left royal life to meditate with his wife, Sita, in the forest. She was kidnapped by the demon Ravan and brought to Ceylon. Rama, his brother and the monkey god Hanuman followed and after many adventures the couple were reunited and ruled their kingdom in peace. Possibly based on some historical foundations, Rama became an avatar of Vishnu who destroys sin and brings deliverance from trouble while Sita is an example of purity.

The *Bhagavad-Gita* or 'Song of Krishna' is very popular and accepted as god's word because Krishna is an important incarnation of Vishnu. It can be translated as 'The Song of the Adorable One' and is the sixth book of the *Mahabharata*, the world's longest poem, although some scholars consider it of later construction dating from 200BC-200AD. The *Bhagavad-Gita* takes the form of a dialogue between prince Arjuna and his charioteer Krishna, an incarnation of the supreme god Vishnu. The setting is the Battle of Kurukshetra where Arjuna wants to back down as he is aware the planned battle will involve killing many of his relatives. Krishna explains that it is Arjuna's *dharma* to fight, *dharma* being the custom or religious duty that cannot be avoided. Following *dharma* is one of the poem's main themes. Other themes include *bhakti* or loving devotion to God and God's love, *samkhya* (theory) providing the analysis of reality and *yoga* (practice) showing the means of attainment. *Karma* or actions that need to be performed are mentioned as a duty. The focus of the poem is Krishna and devotion to him, which involves the observance of dharma. The polytheism of the Vedas was replaced by the pantheism of the *Upanishads* and developed into the possible monotheism of the *Mahabharata*.

Three ways of salvation are revealed:
1. the way of knowledge of the Vedas (mainly for Brahmins)
2. the way of *karma* or works
3. the way of *bhakti* or personal devotion which is open to all irrespective of caste or sex and which is viewed as the best way.

The *Laws of Manu* (200BC) spell out a system to order every detail of daily life and was dharma codified, while *Sutras* are short pieces originating from influential gurus and dealing with specific topics. Perhaps the *Karma Sutra* is the one that has most captured the Irish imagination.

Hindu sacred literature has no end and is being continually updated. Many Hindus consider Gandhi's commentary on the *Bhagavad-Gita* to be inspiring while the nineteenth century words of Sri Ramakrishna are treasured. Even the words of Prabhupada, the founder of ISKCON, are popular beyond the specific followers of that movement. Some will want to study to understand, others will feel the spoken words have a power as in a mantra.

Hindu Divinity
The search for *Brahman*, Eternal Being or Reality is the preoccupation of the Hindu mind and to achieve this goal they are willing to renounce the world, family and comfort and go on arduous pilgrimages. Some Hindu schools believe in a personal god, others in an abstract Reality or energy, with the physical world viewed as illusion. Most Hindus accept the notion of an all-pervading God and while personal devotion will be offered to a particular deity, that deity may be understood as a representative of a particular characteristic or aspect of the one God. They might refer to God as Bhagwan. This perspective con-

siders Hinduism monotheistic and should be viewed as argument rather than accepted fact. In this opinion the supreme spirit or Brahman is the ultimate source and the one supreme reality is impersonal energy, possibly more related to monism than monotheism. Consequently the various gods are explained as representations of the characteristics of *Brahman*. An alternative view sees millions of competing or complimentary gods in a totally polytheistic environment and individuals simply choose their preference – the ultimate consumer society. A more accurate description may be that Hinduism is transtheistic or beyond god.

God always creates out of something or out of himself, never from nothing. Even in the later *Upanishads* and the *Bhagavad-Gita*, where the idea of a personal God is developed, God always tends to be identified with the sum total of creation. The world has neither beginning nor end but is part of an evolutionary cyclical process. These periods are known as 'the days and nights of *Brahman*'. Each day and night lasts 1000 years and each god year equals 12,000 human years. Each year of the gods is divided into four periods of varying length and we are currently living in the fourth or *Kali* age. This is the worst age, started in 3102 BC and will last for 432,000 years. A juggling of modern physics can produce some interesting comparisons with dates. Creation is a transit from chaos to order that may or may not involve a Creator God. It can be viewed as the union of primeval male and female, or the birth of the golden seed. The question as to why there is a constant process of recreation is answered as the sport of God.

Broadly speaking, Hindus may be classified into three groups with reference to devotion to god:

1. those who worship Vishnu and Lakshmi, or Vishnu's important incarnations such as Rama, Krishna and Narasimha

2. those who worship Shiva in the form of lingnam or Nataraja (cosmic dancer)

3. those who worship Shakti the Mother Goddess, variously termed Parvati, Mahalakshmi, Ambaji, Durga or Kali

There is also a trinity of sorts with Brahma (creation), Vishnu (sustaining) and Shiva (destruction) although the specific worship of Brahma has almost disappeared.

Vishnu was a minor deity of light in the Vedas but in modern Hinduism he has come to represent the Preserver aspect of *Brahman*. Often depicted resting on a lotus or under the coils of the serpent Shesha, he is usually represented as having a dark bluish complexion, four hands and riding an eagle. Vishnu preserves or protects the universe and is considered to have appeared on earth in the form of twenty-two avatars or incarnations to save humanity in times of crisis. These avatars include Varaha the boar who destroyed the demon Hiranyaksha, Vamana the dwarf who tricked the demon king Bali, Rama whose deeds of valour against Ravana, king of Lanka are described in the *Ramayana*, Krishna who destroyed the wicked, protected the righteous and established a new world order (*dharma*), Buddha the founder of Buddhism and the last avatar Kalki who is still to come as a rider on a white horse at the end of the present 'Age of Darkness'.

Lakshmi appears in her avatars as the partner to the Vishnu avatars. Consequently she is Padma to Vamana, Sita to Rama and Rukmini to Krishna. Shown as a beautiful woman with four arms rising from a lotus, two hands hold lotus flowers, one hand gives wealth in gold coins and one hand blesses devotees. As goddess of wealth and good fortune she is offered special worship on the Lakshmi-puja day during the Diwali festival.

The pre-Aryan people of the Indus valley worshipped a male god who is pictured crossed legged surrounded by animals. Shiva appears to have grown out of this concept and contains many seeming contradictions. He lives in Mt Kailasa in the Himalayas, has 1008 names and his consort is Parvati and other representations of Shakti (mother goddess). As Nataraja (Lord of the Dance) he is the god of movement in the universe and destruction, yet he is also the god of regeneration and sexuality and usually depicted with one foot on the demon of ignorance and the other foot raised. As Mahayogi he is the god of asceticism and pictured naked with matted hair and ash; associated with evil he is believed to have a third eye with which he destroyed the god of love.

Shakti is worshipped under many names, stressing her various attributes such as mother goddess and loving wife in Parvati, and terror and bloodshed in Kali or Durga. These goddesses are worshipped in their own right and not just as the consort of male gods. The term Shakti can refer to the female goddess in principal, to any goddess or specifically to the wives of Shiva, and is linked to yoga.

The numerous other gods include Ganesha, the son of Shiva and Parvati, who had his head cut off in a misunderstanding by Shiva and was given an elephant head. He is the leader of the *ganas* or semi-divine attendants and worshipped as a god of good luck, wisdom and one who overcomes difficulties. Prayers are offered to Ganesha at the beginning of a *puja*, at life cycle rituals dealing with marriage, entering and leaving homes and when faced with problems. Ganesha is depicted with a pink body and elephant's head with one tusk, riding on or attended by a rat.

Hanuman the monkey chief is the son of Vayu (wind god) and Anjana (semi divine). Renowned for his heroic feats as a helper of Rama, he possesses great strength and agility and the ability to change his shape.

While there are main or prominent gods who can be viewed, to some extent as national or international gods, in villages it is often a very localised deity that will be worshipped. Most of these are female and considered the guardians of the village. The functions of these deities are to give children, food, and overcome sickness and difficulties. There may be other shrines in villages to demons and offerings will be made at these to appease and ward off bad luck. Within Ireland Hindus may have devotion to a minor god from their family or village background, even if several generations ago, and to one or more of the more prominent deities.

Hindu Doctrine

Karma is action or doing and is a moral interpretation of the natural law of cause and effect, extended to the realm of the spirit and to life past, present and future. It applies to good and bad actions; bad actions lead to suffering, good actions lead to freedom from suffering.

Reproductive *karma* is the force of the actions we do which have the power to determine rebirth. Supportive *karma* is the actions that support the reproductive *karma* and can make life pleasant. Counteractive *karma* obstructs reproductive *karma* resulting in suffering. Destructive *karma* stops the flow of the other forces and so a past action may result in an early death even though there was much other good *karma*.

Much of the teaching concerning *dharma* is found in the *Laws of Manu*, dating from around the time of Christ. It is concerned with the general *dharma* or duty placed on all and the specific duty to those from certain castes or arising from relationships. Each has to perform the tasks assigned to them; what is right and wrong is discerned from scripture, other inspired writings, good conduct and conscience. The four separate orders of student, householder, hermit and ascetic are considered and each has certain duties. Each must carry out their own *dharma* and not seek that of another.

Samsara is rebirth or transmigration of the soul. In some ways the soul is identical with *Brahman*, but migrates from body to body, carrying its load of *karma*. This is a natural principle of the universe amongst all people and animals. Due to a person's actions they may be reborn as a god, in a different human caste or as an animal. An individual gets exactly what he or she deserves.

Moksha is the goal for a Hindu: finding release from the endless cycle of rebirth and attachment to the material world and attaining peace. There are two traditional theories to explain how this 'grace' operates:

1. kitten – as a mother cat carries the passive kitten so all is done by God, with nothing by the individual.

2. monkey – this baby clings on to its mother and so there must be a human part in salvation.

This liberation is often seen as merging into *Brahman* rather than reaching a 'heaven'-like state. It comes by knowledge, devotion and action and can be experienced in this life or at death.

One of the strongest distinguishing characteristics of traditional Hinduism has been strict adherence to caste, a closed and rigid social group based on heredity. Caste origins are uncertain, with a pre-Aryan source possible, but it appears to have grown in significance with the multi-racial and multi-cultural nature of India. In marriage, eating and finding employment, caste is a major determining feature. A creation myth describes the origin of caste as resulting from the division of the original man. His mouth was the *brahmins,* arms were the *kshatryas* and warriors, thighs the *vaisyas* and the feet were the *sudras.* Hence the four main caste divisions:

Brahmins – priests and religious teachers	(5% of Hindu population)
Kshatryas – kings and warriors	(6%)
Vaisyas – traders	(6%)
Sudras – farmers and servants	(40%)

Within these groups there are about three thousand *jati* or sub groups based on profession and occupation. Beyond the four castes exist the untouchables or *Dalits.* Several Hindu reform movements have attempted without success to eliminate this distinction. Within India this community is given extra educational and other opportunities by the government, but still suffers very significant disadvantages. In former generations there were mass movements to Christianity; in more recent years movements have been towards Buddhism, such as through Ambekdar. In 2001 there was another significant mass movement of many thousands of *Dalits* into Buddhism.

There could be a new caste emerging at present. Some Indian cities, such as Bangalore, have very large Information Technology

industries and a well paid, highly educated middle class of
many millions has been developing. In some ways this 'caste' is
open to anyone who works in modern industry and falls into a
roughly 'middle class' typology. It is too early to consider this
the beginning of the end for caste, but it is an interesting development.

Worship

The Hindu concept of worship is as varied as the differing expressions of Hinduism. No one word encompasses worship, but
the closest may be *puja* that includes ritual worship but is also
offered to parents and teachers. In this context *puja* can be interpreted as either worship or offering respect. Most Hindu rituals
take place in the home and are generally carried out by women.
These include life-cycle rituals and regional festivals celebrating
specific deities and those of national appeal such as Divali or
Holi.

Devotion offered to an image is not considered as idolatry as
the image is not the deity but rather a symbol and so devotees
are praying to or worshipping the deity personified by the
image. A simple stone can be as effective as an elaborately
carved statue. When a statue is being carved the final moment,
when the pupils are added, is known as the opening of the eyes.
Some consider this is when some aspect of the divinity enters
the statue and part of the power of the divinity is taken on.

Prayer usually consists of the repetition of a mantra a specific
number of times, sometimes helped by prayer beads. Usually
prayers are for one's own state as to pray for others may be to attempt to interfere with their *karma*. In an Irish home the household shrine will usually be an alcove in a wall or a cupboard
which will contain images of particular gods to which offerings
and prayers may be offered daily. It may contain a small lamp
and/or joss stick, gains of rice, flowers and powders such as
turmeric. Similar shrines will also be common in Hindu run
shops, offices and even vehicles.

A more elaborate ceremony may take place in the home dur-

ing an annual festival. That ceremony may involve an invocation where rice grains sprinkled on a statue (*murti*), or grains
may be spread in a copper dish below the statue and the murti's
feet touched by a wet flower to wash them. In a symbol of reverence water and mixture of milk, ghee, honey and sugar may be
placed at the *murti*'s mouth, fresh water offered and the *murti*
symbolically bathed with a flower dipped in water and honey.
A red robe draped around the shoulders, a sacred thread
wrapped around and sandalwood paste applied to its forehead
may honour the statue. Flowers and leaves may then be
arranged at the statue's feet, a joss stick and a ghee lamp lit and
waved in front. Food, perhaps of copra and raw sugar, may be
offered, and fruit and coins placed before the murti. Ideally
devotees will circumambulate but, if that is not possible, the
devotee will turn around a number of times. Finally, sweet
foods may be offered to the murti and then shared among devotees, prayers are offered, songs sung and individuals prostrate
themselves before the image.

There are sixteen rites of passage although only some
Brahmin males will experience all sixteen. Many males will experience about ten, women usually six and almost all Hindus at
least three. Regional variations are important but the generally
accepted list includes rites for conception, for a son, naming a
child, first outing, first solid food, boy's first haircut, piercing
upper part of right ear, sacred thread ceremony, starting to learn
the scriptures, end of Vedic education, marriage ceremony,
householder stage, retirement ritual on 60th birthday and finally
cremation.

Annual festivals vary according to regional variations but include the harvest festival of Navanna, the spring festival of Holi
dedicated to Krishna and New Year or Divali when Lakshmi,
the goddess of good fortune, visits every house lit by a lamp.
Often fireworks to celebrate the victory of good over evil will ac-
company this. The extravagant Divali celebrations witnessed in
some British cities with significant Hindu populations are not
yet replicated in Ireland.

Pilgrimages, often condemned by nineteenth century Hindu reformers, are still popular today, especially among rural Hindus in India. Some are small scale and involve a journey on foot of perhaps a couple of hours to a town or city temple. The exertion of the journey enhances the spirituality of the occasion. A whole village traditionally was involved and offerings of flowers, coconut and cash will be brought. The sacred rivers of the Ganges and Godavari, and the sacred cities of Banares, Puri and Hardwar attract huge numbers, sometimes numbering millions for specific festivals. Caste is temporarily suspended during a pilgrimage and all will bathe together in a sacred river. These are the largest gatherings of people for a single purpose on earth. Irish Hindus will return to India to participate in these festivals.

Hindus have been defined as those who accepted the authority of the Brahmin priests and the Vedas. The vast majority of priests come from the Brahmin caste, although the majority of this caste does not enter the priesthood. There is no centralised organisation, rather many priests are attached to a particular temple or, more likely, work only part time as priests.

Sadhus are holy men and women who have taken vows to withdraw from the world. Many live in ashrams were they meditate and follow a very ascetic lifestyle, surviving on the gifts of others. Caste plays no part in this.

Gurus are spiritual guides who may attract followers with their teaching. They can make Hinduism easier to understand and more personal. They will act as advisers to their followers and may claim miracles.

Adaption and Contribution to Ireland

Due to its nature as a collection of related religions without a strict orthodoxy, Hinduism is open to change and development in a way few other faiths are. Many Irish Hindus, perhaps the majority, come from well-educated, urban backgrounds and would tend to follow a more developed form of renaissance Hinduism based around the teaching of gurus. Hindus from a rural village background who have come to Ireland will have diluted the local aspects of their faith. Their devotion to a particular god might be a localised or regional expression that is not found among many of Ireland's Hindus and so a more generalised faith often develops in countries of the Hindu diaspora. Yet this influence can be over-emphasised. Much of Hinduism is expressed within the home and this can remain unaffected by outside factors. Increasing prosperity allows more frequent visits to the areas where the initial immigrants came from, helping to maintain traditional faith expressions. Time will tell if increasing use of the internet will help maintain localised variations or hasten their eradication.

More than is the case for other religions, Ireland has changed the Hinduism of Hindus living here. However, it is not a unique experience for Irish Hindus but rather is a shared experience for most Hindus living in countries other than India. It is hard to see a particular Irish dimension to this 'levelling down' of transplanted Hinduism. What has been emerging over the past fifty years is a form of world or global Hinduism, connected to but distinct from the varieties of Hinduism in India.

In a related way the main Irish Hindu temple, in Belfast, is used for more congregational type worship than is common in India. The temple operates as much as a community centre as a place of worship and while this is not unique to Ireland it is a further example of how Hinduism is adapting to Ireland.

The strength of caste within Hinduism is diminished when Hindus move to countries such as Ireland. Where Hindus form a small minority many of the divisions of caste are overcome. Dietary laws are generally suspended in Ireland but many of the caste restrictions are easily readopted on visits to India or within larger Hindu communities. Caste within Ireland can come to the fore when marriage is contemplated. What Irish may describe as 'arranged marriage' is far from unique to Hinduism but rather is a traditional aspect of South Asian culture embracing Islam, Sikhism and Christianity as much as Hinduism. Irish Hindu parents, who appear to sit lightly on many caste regulations, may still consider the 'ideal' marriage partner for their child to be a Hindu from the same caste group.

Sacred rivers such as the Ganges are very important for Hindus. Living outside of India makes this almost impossible to maintain in any meaningful form but in areas with significant Hindu populations other rivers are being considered, if not as sacred, at least as fulfilling the functions of Indian rivers. In England recent dredging of the Thames has exposed many broken or damaged Hindu statues, the explanation being that these images cannot be destroyed but are to be returned to a sacred river, with the Thames starting to fulfil this role. It is not clear if the Liffey or Lagan are as yet fulfilling this function.

Hindus have made a very significant contribution to the business life of Northern Ireland. Many have established businesses within the clothing industry in Belfast and Londonderry, ranging from small shops to factories. There are many Hindus found in Ireland's medical professions and in recent years Indian-run catering enterprises and hotels have flourished. A minority occupation has been that of cricket professional, with a number of Indian cricketers playing for Irish teams. In the late 1950s the artist Avinash Chandra lived in Belfast, just before his work came to prominence in Europe. In 1965 Chandra became the first British Indian to exhibit at the Tate Gallery in London and by his death in 1991 he had held over thirty individual exhibitions.

There have been numerous instances when Northern Ireland's small Hindu community has suffered during 'the Troubles'. In the 1970s and 1980s Hindu owned shops in Londonderry and Belfast were bombed, not because of the ethnic or religious background of the proprietors but due to the IRA campaign of attacking the general commercial life of the province. That Ulster's Hindus were disproportionately represented in the retail sector led to many suffering attack. The most serious loss to Ireland's Hindu community was the IRA murder of Asha Chopra and her unborn child in Londonderry in 1974. Asha was sitting in her car in stationary traffic caused by a hoax bomb alert when a single shot struck her in the head. It is thought the shot was aimed at a police officer but Asha Chopra and her unborn child were the victims.

An unforeseen consequence of the relative peace enjoyed in Northern Ireland since the mid 1990s has been an upsurge of racist attacks in Northern Ireland, especially in Belfast. It would appear that some of the violence within the two traditional Northern Irish communities, that used to be directed against each other, is now being directed at those who are seen as 'different'. Among these are Northern Ireland's Hindus, some of whom are now third or fourth generation residents but who are suffering sustained attack for the first time. These attacks take the form of intimidation, paint and petrol bomb assaults on homes and businesses and physical assaults on individuals. To her shame Belfast, in the first years of the third Christian millennium, has been labelled the racist capital of Europe.

A further atrocity to affect Ireland's Hindu community was the bombing of an Air India flight from Canada to India. On 23 June 1985 a bomb exploded when the plane was off the south west coast of Ireland killing all 329 passengers and crew. While no Irish Hindus were aboard this flight, the sight of hundreds of bodies being brought ashore was deeply harrowing for Ireland's Hindu community. The Belfast Hindu priest came to administer rites for the dead and a memorial was erected near the village of Ahakista in Co Cork. Memorial events of an inter-faith nature related to this disaster were part of the impetus for some of Ireland's Christian denominations to start to consider the implications of inter-faith worship.

In Britain Hindus are a very significant and visible part of life, particular in London and the midland cities. In Northern Ireland there has been a Hindu population for over fifty years but a Hindu community is only now becoming established in the Republic of Ireland, with a particular influx of medical professionals. Irish Hindus will become more visible in years to come and are to be expected to make the same significant contribution on the business and cultural life of Ireland as they have in Britain.

CHAPTER SIX

Buddhists

Irish Buddhists were thin on the ground in post war Ireland and so there was local interest generated when a 'Dr Tuesday Lobsang Rampa' moved to Howth, Co Dublin in the early 1950s for a few years. He claimed to have met the Dalai Lama and published *Living with the Lama* and *Doctor from Lhasa*. Later he was shown to have been the not so exotic Cyril Hoskins, a plumber from Devon.

Perhaps Ireland's most significant Buddhist encounter was the visit in October 2000 of the Dalai Lama. He is not strictly the leader of world Buddhism. The Dalai Lama is a leader of one of the four main schools of Tibetan Buddhism and political ruler of Tibet. Since the invasion and virtual destruction of Tibet as a nation by China, the Dalai Lama in exile has come to be regarded as *de facto* head of world Buddhism. He visited Belfast to participate in 'The Way of Peace: the John Main Seminar' sponsored by the World Community for Christian Meditation.

History of the Irish Buddhist Community
Ireland has yet to experience a significant ethnic Buddhist community. In the 1970s some Vietnamese families were settled in Craigavon, coming to the UK as asylum seekers, but most of these families stayed only a short time before moving back to Britain. Approximately two hundred Vietnamese came around the same time to the Republic of Ireland and this Irish Vietnamese community had grown to one thousand by the year 2000. However, while a form of Buddhism is the majority faith in Vietnam, most of these immigrants were ethnically Chinese and their religious understanding is considered in Chapter

Seven. A smaller number of these immigrants were Roman Catholics who had been forced from northern to southern Vietnam in the 1950s and forced to move again a generation later. A small number of Sri Lankans have recently settled in Ireland, although this community comprise Hindu and Christian as well as Buddhist.

Currently Buddhism exists in Ireland largely through Irish converts to Buddhism rather than as an immigrant community. Converts may be too strong a word, as most of these Irish are followers of particular meditative practices rather than devotees in the sense that a Sri Lankan or Thai may be a Buddhist. In 2005 twenty-four small groups were found throughout the Republic of Ireland, operating more as teaching and meditation centres than places of worship for a faith community. These groups are active in inter-faith events, their presence helping to show an increasing acceptance of alternative religious practices in Irish society. They receive inquiries from Irish people of nominally Christian background who are looking to investigate alternative spiritual paths.

The oldest of these various Buddhist centres is the Kagyu Samye Dzong Buddhist Centre in Kilmainham, Dublin. Founded in 1977 as an outreach from a monastery in Scotland, the main programme consists of weekly meditation sessions, courses on philosophy and contemplation and Buddhist worship. In the same area of Dublin the Tara Buddhist Centre was founded in 1993 by the Venerable Geshe Kelsang Gyatso. He can be considered as a sort of Tibetan Buddhist Billy Graham, as Gyatso has established Kadampa Buddhist centres throughout Europe over the past thirty years. His goal is to see a Buddhist centre established in every major world city. The current resident teacher is Kelsang Yonchen, a Buddhist nun. The Dublin Buddhist Centre on Lower Leeson Street draws its roots from another variety of Tibetan Buddhism. The largest group in Ireland is currently Rigpa Ireland, teaching a further variety of Tibetan Buddhism with centres in Athlone, Cork, Dublin, Galway, Killarney, Limerick and Delgany.

To the outsider the proliferation of different Buddhist expressions in Ireland can seem like different Christian denominations – not in opposition to each other but still aware of their differences. Drawing on a Japanese tradition the Irish Zen group has meditation centres in Dublin, Galway, Cork and Navan. The main teacher is Alain Liebmann, a Buddhist monk originally from France. Currently based in Galway he settled in Ireland in 1991 and is in demand throughout Europe as a Zen teacher. While Buddhist centres are more common in the Republic of Ireland, groups do exist in Northern Ireland reflecting the various traditions, for example a Thai Theravada meditation group meets in Newry. In the Northern Irish census of 2001 the figure of 533 Buddhists is not reflected by regular Buddhist worship. Buddhist communities suggest there are no more than fifty Buddhists in Northern Ireland. The difference may be understood as members of the ethnic Chinese community describing their faith as Buddhist, or even some respondents seeking to mislead the census – something of a recent Northern Irish tradition. The 2002 census figure for the Republic of Ireland was 3,894.

What may be more visible to Irish people, more than the small meditation groups in the cities, are the small number of Buddhist retreat centres. Examples include Passaddhi, a centre outside Adrigole on the Beara Peninsula overlooking Bantry Bay. In the same area is Dzogchen Beara from the Rigpa Ireland tradition. Jampa Ling was established in 1990 in County Cavan in a large Victorian house called Owendoon, while the Tashi Khyil Tibetan Buddhist Centre, started in the same year, is situated near Crossgar, Co Down. All these centres offer courses in meditation and Buddhist teaching and are available for individuals to use for their own personal retreats. Taking the Sunday afternoon drive through some of Ireland's most beautiful areas enables you to stumble across Buddhist temples in the most unexpected areas.

WHAT IS THE IRISH BUDDHIST FAITH?

It is useful to note that the word 'Buddhism' can be considered as a western invention; eastern adherents are more likely to talk of *Dharma*. Buddhism can also be read, to some extent, as a 'protestant' reaction against the practice of Hinduism two and a half thousand years ago, and problems that included the expense of sacrifices for participants and the caste system.

Foundation

The founder of Buddhism was not a god, prophet or messiah but rather a normal human being who, by his own efforts, became completely awake, both to his own potential and to the nature of the world around him. The Buddha was born as Siddhartha Gautama in the Terai lowlands near the foothills of the Himalayas just inside the borders of modern day Nepal, about 230 miles north of Benares. He traditionally lived from 566-486BC, and as such he was a contemporary of Pythagarus and Nehemiah although some research would like to place Gautama about 70 years earlier. Discovering 'the historical Buddha' is a difficult task but the following is an approximation of the Buddha's final life.

Siddhartha Gautama was born into a wealthy and noble Hindu Shakya family, probably from the second or warrior caste. Married at sixteen, Gautama left home at twenty-nine, became enlightened at thirty-five and spent the next forty-five years as a wandering teacher. More correctly we should talk of births as the Buddha had many existences going back millions of years and enjoying lives as men, animals and gods. The *Jataka* contains five hundred and fifty birth stories and details of these previous lives. Texts describe how the Buddha was conceived when his mother Maya dreamed that a white baby elephant entered her side, a dream that was interpreted to mean she would bear a son who would be either a great emperor or else a great religious teacher. His mother travelled to her hometown for the birth and she went into labour and gave birth standing up holding on to the trunk of a Sal tree. The gods came to view and the ground shook when the child was laid on the ground. The baby was bathed in a miraculous shower of water, stood up and took seven steps and declared that this would be his last birth. Seven days later the Buddha's mother died and he was raised by his mother's sister, Mahapatjapati. His mother's death is explained as her life being fulfilled once she had given birth to the Buddha.

The Buddha's father wished to protect him from any of life's realities that might cause Gautama to consider the place of religion so that his son would remain in the palace and become King. On rare journeys outside of the palace the king arranged for only healthy, happy people to be seen. However, despite the luxury and comfort, the Buddha found his life unfulfilling. On either one trip or four successive journeys outside of the palace he saw an old man, a sick man, a corpse about to be buried and finally a religious ascetic. These experiences caused him to reflect on his life and the meaning of suffering and decay. On the night he saw the ascetic the Buddha left his sleeping wife and son (Rahula, meaning chain) and never returned to them, although Mara, the Tempter, tried to get him to return.

The Buddha's decision to leave his family and go in search of spiritual truth has a long tradition in north India and the samana movement, a counter-culture of homeless religious mendicants, was already well established by this time. So he was one among many following a similar path. Gautama had five companions on his search and had as his first teacher Alara Kalama who introduced him to meditation techniques that induced a profound trance. The Buddha mastered this but found it unsatisfying due to its temporary nature.

A second meditation teacher, Uddaka Ramaputta, helped the Buddha to enter into a state of 'neither perception or non-perception'. Again, while this was appreciated, it did not offer the satisfaction that he needed. Gautama's alternative approach was to attempt a vigorously austere lifestyle. First there was breath control, but this only produced headaches. Next, food consumption was reduced to an absolute minimum but soon the Buddha could barely sit and his hair started to fall out. This convinced him that these extremes were unproductive and helped him later formulate his 'middle way' doctrine, a path of moderation where appetites were neither denied nor excessively indulged. His five friends left him, thinking he had gone soft.

Returning to food Gautama began to meditate once more and in the course of one full moon night, while seated under a large pippila tree that would become known as the Bodhi tree, by the banks of the River Niranjana he attained enlightenment. First he was able to look back through his previous lives; next he was able to see the death and rebirth of all types of beings in the universe according to their good and bad deeds. After this he attained the knowledge that his spiritual defilements had been eliminated and that he had overcome his desires and lack of knowledge. Thus he attained *nirvana* and escaped from the process of rebirth, just as he prophesied at his birth. Legend has a cosmic battle raging between various gods and demons attempting to help or hinder Gautama attaining enlightenment. For part of the time he was protected by a giant snake that coiled around him. Gautama also experienced many temptations to give up this path, but persevered, events commemorated at Vesak.

The gods convinced the Buddha to spread his teaching or dharma throughout the world. Supernaturally he realised his former teachers had died but that at Benares on the Ganges he would find his five former associates. These five reluctantly welcomed him and in the Royal Deer Park the Buddha preached his first sermon in which he outlined the essential teachings of Buddhism, known as the 'discourse setting in motion the wheel of truth'. One of the audience immediately glimpsed the truth and entered the stream leading to enlightenment, and eventually the other four joined him. They became monks, were ordained and during the second sermon all achieved enlightenment becoming known as *arahats* or those who attain *nirvana*. The term Buddha was reserved for those who discover the way for themselves. Soon there were sixty *arahats* and the Buddha commissioned them to take the message to the world. Five years later an order of nuns was established. Among the converts were his father, former wife, son and his nephew Ananda who became his companion and helper for the next thirty-five years.

Throughout the rest of his life the Buddha wandered through towns and villages of north-east India, in a area smaller than Ireland. As he engaged in debates and discourses the number of converts grew. One tradition has it that when a prince sent one thousand troops to welcome the Buddha they were all converted and became monks. A further one thousand were sent with the same result until the prince could not afford to loose any more soldiers and there were ten thousand new monks. Miracles were ascribed to the Buddha due to the supreme psychic powers he developed and eventually residential centres or *viharas* were established where the monks would spend the rainy season. While there was much acceptance of his message, at least three attempts on his life appear to have been made.

When aged eighty and in failing health the Buddha explained to Ananda that he was not to have a successor as he never saw himself as head of an order, rather the *dharma* should be the guide. The Buddha died at a small town called Kusinara, lying between two Sal trees that miraculously bloomed out of season. He had suffered from food poisoning just before this but seems to have died of natural causes. Before his death the Buddha had asked his monks if they had any questions, and when three times in succession there were none he presumed that the *dharma* had been fully explained. His last words were, 'Decay is inherent in all component things. Work out your salvation with diligence.' Ananda declared that the Buddha was dead, but was corrected by a monk who declared that, rather than dead, the Buddha had now entered into the state where both sensations and ideas have ceased to be.

The Buddha's remains were cremated – tradition has it that much of this ash took the form of diamond – and the remains were enshrined in a bell-like structure called a *stupa*, in a similar way to a king. *Stupas* and statutes of the Buddha are ever-present sights in Buddhist countries.

Development

From the outset Buddhism was a missionary religion and the Buddha showed that in his own life by constantly travelling for the forty-five years after his enlightenment to spread his message. He had a significant impact in northern India during his lifetime but the major growth occurred through the influence of Ashoka.

Ashoka became king of India around 268BC and through conquest he extended the Mauryan Empire, making it the largest Indian empire until the British era. After a very vicious campaign in Orissa in eastern India, he became remorseful about the cost in life and suffering and turned to Buddhism. He ruled according to Buddhist principles, established the faith throughout India and sent ambassador/missionaries to other countries such as Burma and Thailand, Cambodia, Laos and Vietnam to help spread the faith. His brother Mahinda was sent to Ceylon where he founded a monastic settlement at the capital of Anuradhapura in 250BC. Ambassadors were sent westwards but there is no documentary evidence that any reached Ireland.

Buddhism in India flourished for the first half of the millennium but by the year AD1000 Buddhism was in decline and at the end of the tenth century Muslim Turks were able to easily attack the unfortified monasteries. In 1192 a Turkish tribe established rule over northern India and soon Buddhism had virtually died out in the region. The five million Buddhists found today in India are more recent Dalit converts from Hinduism, largely as a reaction against caste restrictions.

In 83BC the *Pali* canon of scripture was first written down on palm leaves, and Sri Lankan Buddhists consider that they have a special task to preserve and promote Buddhism throughout the world. Buddhism spread to China from India by the first century of the Christian era through evangelist monks who travelled along the silk route. Buddhism was considered by some to carry on from where Confucianism ended, especially concerning death and the afterlife, and soon many Chinese held both faiths, one dealing with this world and the other with the next.

Buddhism reached a high point under the T'ang dynasty (AD618-907) and remained as an influential portion of the mixture that is Chinese religion. The post World War II communist take over and the 1966 Cultural Revolution placed Buddhism under great pressure, although it has survived and remains particularly strong in Taiwan.

Buddhism came to Japan in the sixth century via Korea but drew much of its inspiration from China. In 593 the ruler became a student of Buddhist and Confucian scriptures and traditional Shintoism was fused with Buddhism. In 1868 a revolution rejected Buddhism because of its close association with dictators but since 1875 there has been freedom of religion.

Various Japanese approaches to Buddhism have emerged such as Pure Land and Zen. There has been a strong social engagement and monks marry and take a full part in community life. Zen Buddhism stresses meditation in a calm and relaxed rather than philosophical way, giving significance to various art forms. Doctrinal formulations are not particularly important.

Due to the almost inaccessible nature of Tibet, Buddhism only entered in the eighth century and has taken a particular form known as Mantrayana due to the use of magical formulas and chants. Rich symbolism and various unique religious practices augment Mahayana philosophy. Lamas teach devotees hidden meanings to various magic circles, pentagrams, spells and charms. Tantric teachings can be understood on many levels and various schools developed secret practices. Desire is no longer considered a problem but is harnessed for positive means. The Dalai Lama encompasses both the religious and political worlds and ruled Tibet since 1642 until the current incumbent fled in 1959, nine years after the Chinese invasion. Since the invasion Buddhism has been systematically persecuted by the Chinese as it is seen as representing the cultural and religious heart of Tibet, a process carried out in order to hasten the destruction of Tibet as a country. Most modern maps no longer show Tibet.

There is a small Irish connection with the Dalai Lama in that his nieces were educated at a Loreto Convent in India run by Irish nuns. More importantly the Tibetan cause at the UN was raised by Ireland and Malaya in 1959 provoking a debate, much to the displeasure of China and Russia.

Buddhism began to gain a following in western countries in the nineteenth century, significantly helped by the publication of the epic poem *The Light of Asia* by Sir Edward Arnold chronicling the life of the Buddha. In 1924 Christmas Humphries founded the Buddhist Society in England and two years later the Maha Bodhi Society was founded and a monastery established for Sri Lankan monks. Scholars were attracted to the Theravada form of Buddhism but in more recent years Zen and Tibetan Buddhism have become influential.

Beliefs

The Buddha's teaching was preserved by his disciples and transmitted orally through the next few generations. There were three general councils in the period from 483BC-225BC when many points of doctrinal dispute were clarified. Finally in 83BC King Vattagamani Abhaya of Sri Lanka had the scriptures written down on palm leaves in the Pali language, traditionally in three parts known as the *Tipitaka* or Three Baskets.

The *Vinaya Pitaka* deals mainly with rules and regulations for the monks and nuns. The *Sutta Pitaka* consists of discourses delivered by the Buddha and some of his more distinguished disciples. This includes the *Dharmapada* containing 423 verses of ethical instruction and the *Jataka* containing events in the previous lives of the Buddha. The *Abhidhamma Pitaka* contains the profound philosophy behind the Buddha's teaching. It analyses phenomena, explaining the nature of mind and matter.

The idea and practice of the three Jewels is central to Buddhists, perhaps having the same place as the *Shahada* within Islam. Buddhists affirm that they take refuge in the Buddha, the dharma and the *Sangha*, or community of Buddhism.

The Buddha was able to recall numerous past lives in considerable detail and Buddhism understands an almost endless succession of rebirths known as *samsara* or endless wandering. All living creatures are part of this cyclic process and will continue to be reborn until they obtain *nirvana*. Hindu concepts underpin much of this area of Buddhism. The main difference between the two faiths is that Buddhism does not recognise a soul that moves from one body to another. Rather it is the consequence of a person's *karma* that transmigrates.

Buddhist thought divides the universe into two categories: the physical universe and the beings that inhabit it. The physical universe is formed by the interaction of earth, water, fire, air and space. Their interaction forms world systems (like galaxies) in six directions (north, south, east, west, up and down). These systems undergo cycles of evolution and decline lasting for billions of years. The quality of lives of the inhabitants partially determines how long the galaxy survives. A creation story in the *Agganna Suta* tells of the inhabitants of a destroyed world system being reborn as translucent creatures in a new evolving system. As the fabric of this world solidifies these creatures start to eat and consume it and become more physical. In order to regulate this they elect a king and so a new society is begun. This shows the origins of human suffering in desire.

In the Buddhist cosmology, hell is a place of torment and terrible suffering, both hot and cold, but is only temporary and when the bad *karma* has been used up then there is release. The animal realm is not much of an improvement due to their poor quality of life. The ghosts have only a shadowy existence around the edges of the human world. They were too attached to the human world by their desires and now still have these same desires but can no longer fulfil them. Titans are demonic warlike creatures at the mercy of violent impulses seeking conquests in which they find no satisfaction. The human world is a desirable place in which to be reborn and offers a middle way between pleasure and suffering. It also offers the possibility of much further advancement. Beyond this the twenty-one levels of the gods are wonderful, long lasting existences but it is possible to slip back and be reborn at a lower level. The final five levels or Pure Abodes are for the non-returners who cannot return to the human sphere but will soon attain enlightenment.

Karma is what determines the destination of the individual. Basically, good deeds result in upward movement and bad deeds in downward movement. Rather than a system of divine rewards, *karma* is a natural law that involves the moral value of an action as much as the action itself. The moral choices we make help to form our character. Not all the consequences of our actions happen in this life, but can be carried forward to the next or subsequent lives. However *karma* does not mean everything in life is determined, there is still much freedom of choice. Actions motivated by greed, hatred and delusion are bad and actions motivated by non-attachment, benevolence and understanding are good. Good intentions need to be translated into good actions to make progress.

Much effort is spent in acquiring good *karma* or merit, somewhat like spiritual capital that is locked away until it is needed later. An effective way of obtaining merit is to help the priesthood by gifts of food, robes, by listening to sermons and financial donation. However, doing good deeds to obtain merit would be to act from a selfish motive and so would have the opposite karmic effect.

Everything is dependent on something else; nothing can arise on its own accord. For example a lamp remains burning because of a wick that depends on oxygen and a sufficient temperature; even oxygen is a combination of elements and a wick is composed of different strands of cotton. This explains the cycle of lives and how a person accumulates *karma* and is reborn through the round of existence as depicted in the 'wheel of becoming' – a wheel of twelve spokes denoting the twelve links of the causal process:
- dependent on ignorance so intentional activities arise
- dependent on intentional activities so consciousness arises
- dependent on consciousness so mental and physical phenomena arise

- dependent on mental and physical phenomena so the six senses arise
- dependent on six senses so contact arises
- dependent on contact so sensation arises
- dependent on sensation so craving arises
- dependent on craving so clinging arises
- dependent on clinging so the process of becoming arises
- dependent on becoming so birth arises
- dependent on birth so decay, sorrow, suffering, pain, grief and despair arise.

The ultimate goal of Buddhism is to put an end to suffering and rebirth. Someone who achieves this complete state of self-realisation is said to have obtained *nirvana*, both a concept and an experience. It offers a particular vision of human fulfilment and becomes real in the life of the seeker.

Leading a good life and gaining merit is only part of the pathway to *nirvana*. This needs to be supplemented by wisdom that involves a profound philosophical understanding of the human condition. This is a long process of thought and reflection that eventually reaches full maturity in the complete awakening experienced by the Buddha. In his first sermon in the Deer Park, the Buddha laid out the wisdom that was needed to obtain enlightenment in four basic concepts known as the Four Noble Truths.

Buddhists consider suffering to be an intrinsic part of life. There is suffering of many kinds but the deeper problem is the repeated birth, sickness, ageing and death in numerous lifetimes. Apart from physical suffering, the realisation that we cannot get what we want is a further type of mental or existential suffering. The Buddha did not accept the concept of an individual soul (*atman*) or its cosmic counterpart (*Brahman*), rather an individual's personal moral identity continues beyond a specific death. There are five factors of humanity and they all involve suffering: the physical body, sensations and feelings, understanding, character traits and consciousness.

Suffering comes from craving or desire. It is desire for life and the pleasant experiences it can offer that causes rebirth. This desire will show itself in three ways – desire for sensual pleasure such as taste or sight, desire for existence, desire to destroy or to reject what is not wanted.

All desire is not wrong. There is positive desire such as that for nirvana and that others should experience happiness. These right desires enhance and liberate – an Irish example might be related to the desire for a cigarette and the desire to give up smoking.

When desire is removed, then *nirvana* is achieved. *Nirvana* takes two forms: in this life, such as the Buddha experienced under the tree, and at death when the final *nirvana* is reached from which a person cannot be reborn. *Nirvana* literally means 'blowing out', such as in a candle, and what is extinguished in nirvana is the greed, hatred and delusion that leads to rebirth. This can be understood in life in a very serene person but it is not so clear at death. It is not annihilation and it is not existence, rather it is an enigma that the Buddha taught was not to be understood but rather to be attained.

An individual passes from the endless wandering of *samsara* to *nirvana* by way of the Noble Eightfold Path:

- right view – accepting the Buddha's teachings
- right resolve – serious commitment to developing right attitudes
- right speech – telling the truth and speaking in a sensitive way
- right action – not acting wrongly or indulging overly in sensual pleasures
- right livelihood – not working where harm could be caused to others
- right effort – controlling thoughts and being positive
- right mindfulness – constant awareness
- right meditation – developing deep levels of mental calm.

This is the Middle Way because it avoids the extremes of indulgence and austerity. The first two involve wisdom, the next three involve morality and the final three involve meditation.

All this is a type of self-transformation process that changes a person intellectually, morally and socially. Through the pursuit of knowledge and moral virtue, ignorance and desire are overcome, the cause of the arising of suffering is removed, and *nirvana* is obtained.

Worship

The common image of the Buddha is of him sitting cross-legged in meditation and it was in this way that Gautama obtained nirvana, part of a process whereby a person makes himself or herself into what they wish to be. The Buddha was familiar with the teachings of the *Upanishads* and that of *Yoga*. What he did was to modify existing practices to suit his understanding.

Meditation can be defined as an altered state of consciousness that is induced in a controlled manner. Daydreams are common to all and show the possibilities of entry into meditation. Types of meditation are found in all religions. In order for the mind to be calm, the body must be composed and the lotus position of sitting cross-legged with the back straight, head slightly inclined and hands in lap is considered helpful. Concentration can be achieved by repeating a silent mantra or focusing on an object. Meditation results in heightened powers of concentration, an inner calm and confidence. Buddhist meditation practices take the individual from detachment to rapture, through peace that leads a person beyond pleasure or pain to an eventual state where there is neither perception nor non-perception. The Buddha did not view meditation as an escape from the world but rather the generation of insight and focus in order to sharpen the intellectual capabilities.

In addition to meditation, there are types of corporate worship such as listening to sermons and veneration of relics and religious symbols. Incense, flowers and prostration will be offered. Often the monks will chant in Pali or Sanskrit, making it difficult for lay people to fully participate. In a similar way to Hinduism, most Buddhist homes will have a household shrine with prayers and offerings of incense being offered daily.

Pilgrimage to places related to the Buddha's life or where relics are held is also popular.

Living the Faith

The Buddha founded the *Sangha* or community soon after his enlightenment, the first five members of the clergy being the five ascetics who were converted after the first sermons in the Deer Park. Admission to the *Sangha* was open to all without any caste restrictions and women were as welcome as men. The *Sangha* has two sections, the first for male and female clergy, the second for laypeople.

The monks generally live in community and often engage in teaching; they take vows of poverty, shave their heads and wear distinctive saffron robes. There is a sliding scale of regulations for the ordained, rising as they progress to a total of 227. In some countries, such as Sri Lanka, the *Sangha* still has significant political influence.

There are five precepts for lay Buddhists: to refrain from harming living beings, from taking what is not given, from sexual misconduct and misuse of the senses, from harmful speech and drink or drugs which cloud the mind. The newly ordained monk promises to follow these and additionally to refrain from eating after midday, from dancing, amusements, singing with instruments, from perfumes and garlands, from sleeping in comfortable beds and from accepting money.

Differences

After the Buddha's death the lack of a central leader resulted in the growth of various schools of interpretation. The most serious disagreement occurred about one hundred years into the Buddhist era between a group later designated as the 'Elders' (*Theravada*) and those known as the 'Universal Assembly' (*Mahayana*). The disagreement probably centred on the Elders' wish to add to the Monastic Rules and was influenced by the question as to whether expanding Buddhism should adapt or not to new beliefs and practices. Further, some emphasised the words of the Buddha to an extent that the spirit of the message could be lost, with a tendency to view the quest for enlightenment as a selfish personal search. Basically, Mahayana is a more liberal, syncretistic understanding that considers the Buddha a saviour whereas Theravada is a more conservative understanding stressing more the teaching rather than the person of the Buddha. Generally a Buddhist country will be overwhelmingly either Mahayana or Theravada although within each expression local identity plays a very significant role.

Mahayana or the 'great vehicle' understands itself as the universal way to salvation. It developed around the time of Christ and Christianity may well have influenced it. The ideal is a life dedicated in service to others, helping others find enlightenment rather than concentrating on oneself, and by showing compassion in practical ways. Rather than just a teacher the Buddha is viewed as having three bodies: the human body he had on earth, a heavenly body located upstream in a blissful realm and a transcendent body identical with ultimate truth. There is a belief that a Buddha, known as Maitreya, will appear at the end of the present age when there will be a utopian era when many will achieve enlightenment.

The nucleus of the Mahayana understanding was a series of new scriptures that appeared in the early years of the Christian era. While not claimed as coming from the Buddha's hand, these texts, written in Sanskrit, claimed the Buddha as their spiritual author. The *Lotus Sutra* argues that while the Buddha appeared as an ordinary man, in reality he was enlightened from all time and went through a charade to help people. He had not fully revealed all his teaching as it was beyond people at the time but now it could be fully revealed. He was a type of 'Superman' who could perform many miracles and brought salvation both by his teaching and also in his person. There are other canons of Mahayana teaching that compliment these *Sutras* such as the Tibetan Canon that includes *The Tibetan Book of the Dead* and various Chinese writings.

The path to salvation begins with a moment of enlightenment that could be considered like a conversion experience. Then a vow is taken to lead others to *nirvana*, no matter how long this takes. As the Bodhisattva practises six virtues or Perfections he/she advances through ten stages towards nirvana. These virtues, which can be considered as a reformulation of the Noble Eightfold Path, include generosity, morality, patience, courage, meditation and wisdom. Bodhisattvas who had reached the higher stages of their careers were visualised as enormously powerful beings, virtually identical to the Buddha in his heavenly form. The Tibetan Dalai Lamas are said to be incarnations of the celestial Bodhisattva 'Avalokitesvara' or 'the Lord who looks down in compassion'. A rich pantheon of Buddhas and Bodhisattvas come into being, inhabiting a majestic, unseen universe. A family of five Buddhas became popular. Pure Land Buddhism comes from one of these Buddhas called Amida who took a vow that if he obtained enlightenment he would assist any that called on his name in faith to be reborn in the Pure Land.

Mahayana has a doctrine of emptiness whereby objects do not have any substance in themselves beyond what makes them up. Consequently there is no such thing as a chair; rather there are legs, a back, a seat and so on. This was expanded to consider that all phenomena or people and things are empty of any real being and so was a middle way between existence and non-existence. Therefore there is no difference in substance between *nirvana* and the cycle of rebirth. Any difference lies in our perception. Consider a man who is frightened by a coil of rope thinking it is a snake. To liberate us in life, correct vision seeing things as they really are is needed. *Nirvana* is here and now if we could but see it.

Mahayana reinterprets rather than rejects the early teaching of the Buddha with Theravada claiming to have recovered the true meaning.

Theravada	*Mahayana*
men/women as individuals	men/women as involved with others

Theravada	*Mahayana*
individuals are on their own	men/women are not alone
emancipation by self effort	salvation by grace
key virtue – wisdom	key virtue – compassion
religion – a fulltime job	religion – relevant to life in the world
primarily for monks	for lay and monks
ideal is the arahat	ideal is the Bodhisattva
Buddha is a saint	Buddha is a saviour
few rituals	many rituals
prayer as meditation	petitionary prayer
conservative	liberal

Zen Buddhism is an intuitive, experimental school of Mahayana Buddhism that spread from India to China and then on to Japan where it became prominent. The legendary transmitter of Zen was Bodhidharma, 28th Patriarch of Mahayana Tradition and 1st Zen Patriarch. However it was Hui-neng in the sixth century AD who gave Zen its distinctive characteristics. Since his time Zen has sub-divided into a number of schools. Zen's most influential time was from the thirteenth to the sixteenth centuries during which it became the religion of the Samurai ruling classes. Its affirmation of the world made it a driving force in education, government, trade and culture. In the twentieth century D. T. Zuzuki introduced Zen to the west.

The key to Zen thought and experience is enlightenment. Humanity's basic problem is ignorance about the true reality of the world and in our attempt to understand reality intellectually we miss the direct experience of life. What Zen teaches is a distinctive intuitive insight into reality or the Buddha nature that is identical with our mind so that enlightenment comes by insight into the Buddha nature and our own self. Enlightenment is the acquisition of a new viewpoint that leads to a new way of life.

Any technique that that leads to enlightenment is valid and care is taken not to replace the goal of enlightenment with a technique. The Rinzai school looks to shock the disciple from his/her old way of thinking by use of a sudden shouted answer or even physical hit. Another popular way is by the use of *koans* – a rationally insoluble riddle posed by a master to a pupil such as 'what is the sound of one hand clapping?' There are approximately 1700 *koans* and a pupil may meditate for years on one before a sudden flash of intuition brings enlightenment.

Tibetan Buddhism consists of five main schools with numerous subdivisions, all holding the main mahayana teachings in common with some small variations. What separates Tibetan Buddhism from other forms is *tantra*, a teaching to help people link to the Buddha and discover harmony. It is necessary to learn this from a spiritual teacher, with the oral transmission considered vital.

Adaption and Contribution to Ireland
Apart from the very few Buddhist buildings on the Irish landscape, the lack of a large or ethnic Buddhist community has limited Buddhist impact on Ireland.

Yet many Irish are interested in aspects of Buddhism and it is a growing faith in Ireland. The market place of religions is in existence and people are picking and mixing various bits of spirituality that work for them. While there are many more Muslims in Ireland, arguably Buddhism is the non-Christian religion that is making the most impact on the nominally Christian traditional Irish population. Irish are visiting Buddhist centres, taking courses, buying books, practicing mediation and exploring what Buddhism is about. Inter-faith Ireland is a reality, not just as various faith communities established within Ireland but through the absorption of religious understandings and practices from one religion to another.

CHAPTER SEVEN

Bahá'is, Sikhs, Chinese and Humanists in Ireland

Bahá'i

I wonder how many Irish people have been employed by one religious community while simultaneously being a follower and evangelist for another? The answer must be almost none but in Revd George Townshend (1876-1957), a Christian-Bahá'i, there is one fascinating example.

Coming from a wealthy Irish Anglican family, Townshend followed a well trodden road from privileged home via English public school to Cambridge, where he won an athletics blue, before going on to be called to the Irish Bar. His story starts to divert from the norm as his legal career never took off; instead he emigrated to USA and lived the life of a frontiersman in the Midwest. After a religious conversion Townshend was ordained into the American Episcopal Church where, after a short but successful missionary period in Utah, he became a school teacher and then a lecturer in the University of the South, Sewanee, Tennessee.

Townshend returned to Ireland in 1916, not through nationalist fervour, but due to temporarily failing eyesight and a broken engagement. As he was convalescing Townshend received some literature on the Bahá'i faith from the librarian at the university in Sewanee which led to his gradual acceptance of the tenets of the faith and the belief that in the person of Bahá'u'lláh was Christ returned. However, this far from orthodox Christian view did not stop Townshend being appointed Rector of Ahascragh in 1919, a parish he served for twenty-eight years. Townshend formally became a Bahá'i in 1920, eighteen months after taking up his parish appointment. Subsequent progression within the Church of Ireland included serving as Diocesan

Secretary from 1922-1947, being appointed Archdeacon of Clonfert in 1933 and serving as a Canon of St Patrick's Cathedral, Dublin.

Townshend, like many of his class and generation, was a man of letters and started to correspond with the Guardian of the Bahá'i faith. This relationship developed as Townshend became Shoghi Effendi's chief translator, working on most of the major Bahá'i publications over a thirty-five year period. Some of Townshend's own writings became significant Bahá'i statements of understanding, including *The Promise of All Ages*, *Christ and Bahá'u'lláh*, and *The Heart of the Gospel*. While there were many more publications and articles, these three have been translated into numerous languages and are among the most important Bahá'i writings of the twentieth century.

Just how Townshend remained an Anglican cleric while working for the Bahá'i faith is explained by his desire to bring the Church of Ireland into the Bahá'i faith. That this was most unlikely did not daunt him and Townshend looked for opportunities where his public association with the Bahá'i faith might come to prominence and so raise awareness about his new faith. In 1936 Townshend was convinced that his moment had come when he gave a paper on the Bahá'i faith at the Congress of the World Fellowship of Faiths. Unfortunately the 'Edward and Mrs Simpson' affair was breaking and a Church of Ireland Archdeacon with bizarre religious views did not merit any press attention.

A further factor in Townshend's remaining within Anglicanism was his wife's reluctance to accept the Bahá'i faith and an understandable desire to remain in the comfortable lifestyle and financial security that an Anglican parish provided in mid century Ireland. Finally, in 1947, Townshend resigned from the Anglican ministry, forfeited his pension and lived modestly with his wife in a small house in south Dublin, very different to the rectory at Ahascragh. Only in the last few years of his life was he able to devote his full energies to the Bahá'i faith. He attended Bahá'i conventions and conferences where he was feted as a Bahá'i celebrity and while his resignation from the Anglican ministry did not provoke any hoped-for controversy, Townshend's contribution to the advancement of the Bahá'i faith was recognised by his being appointed a 'Hand of the Cause of God' in December 1951. This placed him in a group of less than ten Bahá'is worldwide who were charged with giving a spiritual lead to the world Bahá'i community.

From a privileged Dublin upbringing, via the American frontier and Anglican ministry in Utah and Co Galway, Townshend was a senior advocate for the Bahá'i faith for almost forty years, most of this time while employed by the Church of Ireland. Inter-faith Ireland has produced a few interesting characters but possibly none more so than George Townshend, sometime Archdeacon of Clonfert and a world leader of the Bahá'i faith

Townshend was not the first Irish Bahá'i. There was an Irish Bahá'i connection from the very start of the faith, with the Báb, the forerunner of the faith's founder, being treated by an Irish doctor while in prison in Iran in 1848. The first Irish Bahá'i was probably a medical doctor called Frederick W. D'Evelyn, born in Belfast around 1855, who helped welcome 'Abdu'l-Bahá, the 'evangelist' of the Bahá'i faith, on his arrival to San Francisco in 1912. One of the earliest Bahá'is to live in Ireland was Henry Culver, the American Consul in Queenstown (now Cobh) from 1906 to 1910. The first Irish Bahá'i family in Ireland appears to have been the Fforde family who moved from Waringstown to Donegal in the 1920s.

The first congregation or Local Spiritual Assembly was formed in Dublin in 1948, followed by Belfast in 1950 with a national organisation being established in 1972. The community in Ireland now numbers several hundred and is quite widely dispersed, with nineteen assemblies in the Republic of Ireland and eight in Northern Ireland. Only a few dozen members are of Iranian origin, the majority being Irish from a nominally Christian background. The fairly rapid growth of the 1970s, when many of the Irish assemblies were formed, appears to have levelled off. In the Republic of Ireland there were four assemblies in 1971 but by 1982 there were nineteen, the present number.

In 1972 the National Governing Assembly divided to form a National Spiritual Assembly for the Bahá'is of the United Kingdom and a National Spiritual Assembly for the Bahá'is of the Republic of Ireland. Subsequently a regional council was formed with responsibility for the administration of the Bahá'i community in Northern Ireland. Both the National Assembly of the Republic of Ireland and the Bahá'i Council are elected bodies with nine members – both women and men. The Bahá'i Council for Northern Ireland relates to the National Assembly of the Baha'is of the UK. This in its turn is one of over 180 such national bodies, functioning under the guidance of the International Governing Body of the Faith, which also is elected.

WHAT IS THE IRISH BAHA'I FAITH?

The Founder

The title of 'Báb' or 'the door' is given to Mirza Ali Muhammed, born in Persia in 1819. His role was similar to that of John the Baptist in Christianity – not a saviour but rather the precursor. Aged twenty-five, Mirza announced he had a new revelation from God and this would be more fully delivered by the imminent arrival of a new 'Messenger'. The Báb gathered a significant number of followers, enough to cause persecution of this new faith community in Persia. After a six year public ministry the Báb was executed in Tabriz aged thirty.

In 1844, when aged twenty-seven, Bahá'u'lláh, the son of a Persian government minister, became a follower of the Báb. Suffering persecution, it was while in prison that Bahá'u'lláh became convinced he was the messenger who had been foretold. On release from prison Bahá'u'lláh was exiled and he spent the last forty years of his life moving around Iraq, Turkey, Egypt and finally Akka in what is now Israel. Bahá'u'lláh spent these years proclaiming his mission and calling all to recognise the unity of humanity and search for world peace.

History

Before his death Bahá'u'lláh appointed his eldest son 'Abdu'l-Bahá as successor and it was he who oversaw significant world-wide expansion, despite periods of imprisonment and exile. Only free to travel in his later years, 'Abdu'l-Bahá helped establish the faith in Europe and America. After his death in 1921 the leadership passed to his grandson Shoghi Effendi, then a student at Oxford. Shoghi Effendi was the real organiser of the Bahá'i faith, developing small local communities into connected groups able to establish institutions to carry out Bahá'u'lláh's vision. During his thirty-six year control he put in place the mechanism that today provides the administrative control of the faith. This 'Universal House of Justice' is a nine person body elected every five years who are charged with applying the teachings of Bahá'u'lláh to the Bahá'i community and is based in Haifa in Israel. Effendi also translated Bahá'u'lláh's writings in Arabic and Persian into English, helping to make the faith more accessible to a wider constituency. After his death in 1957, Effendi was buried in London and the Universal House of Justice took over leadership of the Bahá'i community in 1963.

Differences

There are no significant divergences within the world Bahá'i faith, currently found in approximately 235 nations, although in very small numbers in many of these countries.

Beliefs of the Bahá'í faith.

The central idea of the faith is that of unity, and Bahá'is seek to re-move barriers of race, gender, and belief. They believe that people should work together for the common benefit of humanity.

All human beings have a soul that lives forever. All human beings are members of a single race, which should soon be united in a single global community. All human beings are different, but equal. There should be no inequality between races or sexes and all religions have the same spiritual foundation, despite their apparent differences.

The Bahá'i religion has a similar understanding to Hinduism in that it accepts other faiths as true and valid. Bahá'is accept the divine nature of the work of Abraham, Moses, Zoroaster, the Buddha, Jesus and the Prophet Muhammad. They believe each one was a further stage in the revelation of God. Other prophets and divine manifestations are also accepted. God is transcendent and cannot be known directly but is revealed through the lives and teachings of his great prophets, the most recent of whom was Bahá'u'lláh.

Bahá'is see themselves as a people with a mission to bring harmony and unity in the world, and this is reflected in their spiritual practice, the main purpose of life for Bahá'is being to know and love God. Prayer, fasting and meditation are the main ways of achieving this and for making spiritual progress. Work performed in a spirit of service to humanity is also considered a form of worship.

The Bahá'i faith has no clergy or sacraments, and only a few rituals: obligatory daily prayers, reciting the prayer for the dead at a funeral and the marriage rite. The emphasis on prayer, meditation and social action in Bahá'i thinking means that congregational worship plays a much smaller part in Bahá'i life than it does in other faiths. Bahá'i services are very simple, with readings from the scriptures, along with interpretations and prayers. Hymns and poetry are allowed, but not common. One person will recite prayers on behalf of everyone present because prayer is seen essentially as a private duty. The main occasion for group worship is the devotional portion of the nineteen day feast.

Personal prayer is the significant part of Bahá'i spiritual life. Bahá'is believe that prayer is conversation with God whereas meditation is akin to a conversation with one's inner spirit. Consequently they believe that it is not the language that is important, but rather the attitude of mind in which prayer is made. Prayer is intended to help Bahá'is get closer to God, so its aim is to change the person who is praying, rather than to change God. The purpose of the obligatory prayers is to cultivate humility and devotion.

There are eleven holy days, of which nine are major holy days. Bahá'is are required to refrain from work on the three special days of Ridvan and all major holy days unless specifically disallowed in their terms of employment. Children are not to attend school if possible. Bahá'is are encouraged not to celebrate the holy days of other religions among themselves.

The Ridvan Festival marks the declaration in the Garden of Ridvan in 1863. Naw-Rúz or new year is celebrated on 21 March, the first day of spring equinox. Every nineteen days, on the evening before the first day of each Bahá'i month, Bahá'is meet in a home or their local Bahá'i centre for a shared meal. The Declaration of the Báb is celebrated 22-23 May from two hours after sunset on the 22nd. The Ascension of Bahá'u'lláh is celebrated on 29 May, commemorated at 3am in the morning. The martyrdom of the Báb is celebrated on 9 July at noon and his birth on 20 October. The birth of Bahá'u'lláh is celebrated on 12 November. The minor days, when work is not suspended, include the day of the Covenant on 26 November and the passing of 'Abdu'l-Bahá on 28 November.

Adaption and Contribution to Ireland
Bahá'is are noted for their promotion of peace and have made a small but significant contribution during the conflict in Northern Ireland. During the OPSAHL commission twelve Bahá'i groups or individuals made submissions.

Education features highly in the Bahá'i community. The George Towshend School was started in 1986 by the Castlereagh Bahá'is to give spiritual and moral education to their children. From the beginning the school has encouraged diversity and welcomes children from all backgrounds with the curriculum based on the teachings of Bahá'u'lláh. In the 1980s the Magherafelt Bahá'i community held meetings with 'all children together' – the founders of the integrated school movement. Bahá'i families promoted the founding of integrated schools in Magherafelt, Enniskillen and Dungannon.

The small Irish Bahá'i community hosted the first

International Bahá'i Conference. Two thousand Bahá'is from around the world came to Dublin in June 1982, one of the very few occasions when a world event for a faith community has been held in Ireland.

On 19 February 2001 a delegation from the Londonderry Assembly paid an official visit to the Guildhall as guests of the Mayor of Derry, Councillor Cahal Crumley, to receive a special award, a 'Quaypin' – a sculpture made from the timbers and structures of the city's old quayside. The citation read, '... an award presented in the new millennium by the Mayor to those who have made a significant contribution to our city and sym-bolise a new departure from the old, divided ways into a new, inclusive city.'

The place of Bahá'is in Ireland was recognised by President Mary McAleese who attended a celebration in 1998 to mark fifty years of Bahá'i worship in Dublin. The Bahá'is form a distinct group whose desire for peace and reconciliation has meant this religious community have been able to make a small but signifi-cant contribution to the life of Ireland.

SIKHS

No, it is not compulsory for Sikh men to wear the turban since it is not considered one of the fundamentals of the faith. Nor does every Sikh have the surname Singh, although many do. Despite being a relatively small religion of Indian origination Sikhs, par-tially due to appearance, are one of the more recognisable reli-gious communities in Ireland. However, that numerical insignif-icance has not insulated Sikhs from Ireland's recent conflict. On 5 September 1981 the IRA murdered three British soldiers, one of whom was a Sikh called Sohan Virdee. The role call continued to include people of almost any religious faith that happened to be in Ireland.

One of Northern Ireland's leading businessmen is Diljit Singh Rana, originally from the Punjab. He came to Northern Ireland in 1966 to work in the hospitality industry and became a property developer and hotelier, founding Andras House Ltd in

1981. Four years later Rana helped establish the Indian Business Forum and was President of the Belfast Chamber of Commerce from 1991-1992. In 2004 he was elected President of the Northern Ireland Chamber of Commerce and appointed the first Indian Honorary Consul for Northern Ireland in the same year. Rana received perhaps the highest honour given to a member of Northern Ireland's Asian community when he was elevated to the House of Lords as Lord Rana in 2004.

History of the Sikh Community in Ireland
There have been Sikhs in Ireland for most of the twentieth century but it was only in 1986 that the first Sikh place of worship was established in Ireland with the conversion of a Dublin cinema into a Gurdwara. However it was in Northern Ireland that Sikhs first made an impact. In the aftermath of World War I some Indians, mostly former members of the British Army and including Sikhs, migrated to Britain, often via East Africa. Of this group a very small number moved on to Northern Ireland. Today the Sikh community includes medical professionals, shop-keepers, those involved in the clothing industry in various capacities and a wide variety of other occupations. It can be misleading to even highlight some occupations where members of a particular religious community are disproportionately found. It almost implies that these are the only occupations carried out by members of a particular tradition. That is clearly not the case, but it is of some social significance if there is an occupational preponderance for certain employments.

    Today the main Sikh community in Northern Ireland is centred around Londonderry. In 1990 the Northern Ireland Sikh Association was formed, followed by the refurbishment of a former school in Londonderry into the Northern Ireland Sikh Cultural and Community Centre.

WHAT IS THE IRISH SIKH FAITH?

Foundation
The Sikh faith began around 1500, when Guru Nanak from the

Punjab began teaching a faith that was distinct from Hinduism and Islam. Nanak had received a revelation telling him that 'there is no Muslim, there is no Hindu'. Nine Gurus followed Nanak, developing the Sikh faith and community. Sikhism was well established by the time of Guru Arjan, the fifth Guru who completed the establishment of Amritsar as the capital of the Sikh world, and compiled the first authorised book of Sikh scripture, the *Adi Granth*. However, during Arjan's time Sikhism was seen as a threat by the Indian state and Guru Arjan was eventually executed for his faith in 1606.

The sixth Guru, Hargobind, fought to preserve the community, then followed a period of relative peace until the time of the Moghal Emperor, Aurangzeb, who used force to make his subjects accept Islam and had the ninth Guru, Tegh Bahadur, executed in 1675. The tenth Guru, Gobind Singh, recreated the Sikhs as a military group of men and women called the *Khalsa* in 1699, with the intention that the Sikhs should be able to defend their faith. Gobind Singh established the Sikh rite of initiation (*khandey di pahul*) and the five 'K's which give Sikhs their unique appearance.

Development
The first military leader of the Sikhs to follow the Gurus was Banda Singh Bahadur who led a successful campaign against the Moghals until he was captured and executed in 1716. In the middle years of the century the Sikhs rose up again, and over the next 50 years took over more and more territory until, in 1799, Ranjit Singh captured Lahore, and in 1801 established the Punjab as an independent state, with himself as Maharaja. He proved an very capable ruler of a state in which Sikhs were still in a minority.

After Ranjit Singh's death in 1839 the Sikh state crumbled, damaged by internal leadership battles and they were finally defeated by the British in 1849. For a while the Sikhs peacefully co-existed with the British, partly because they came to think of themselves as partners of the British rather than as subjects of the Raj. However this changed in April 1919 when British troops, commanded by Ireland's General E. H. Dyer, opened fire causing the Amritsar Massacre discussed in Chapter Two.

At Independence in 1947 the Sikhs were too weak to have their own state and suffered greatly from partition and the huge dislocation of people. The Sikh ambition for independence was something that India would not concede as to do so would have allowed communalism (independent religious groupings) an unbreakable foothold in the politics of what was supposed to be a secular state. However, in 1966, after years of Sikh demands, India divided the Punjab into three, recreating Punjab as a state with a Sikh majority. Yet this did not pacify Sikh anger at what they saw as continuing oppression and the unfair way in which they thought India had set the boundaries of the new state.

As Sikh discontent grew, the conflict gradually changed from political into a violent confrontation between Hindus and Sikhs, with Jarnail Singh Bhindranwale the leader of a Sikh ex-tremist movement. In 1983 Bhindranwale and his supporters took refuge in the Golden Temple at Amritsar, the most revered place in the Sikh world. In June 1984 Indian troops attacked the Golden Temple, killing many and seriously damaging the com-plex. This radicalised many formerly moderate Sikhs who viewed the Indian Prime Minister, Indira Gandhi, as a deliberate persecutor of the Sikh community and faith. Four months after the assault on the Golden Temple Indira Gandhi was assassinated by two of her Sikh bodyguards. Today the Punjab is fairly peace-ful, although the recent rise of Hindu nationalism, with its claim that Sikhism is nothing more than a Hindu sect, has renewed tension.

Beliefs
Sikhs believe that human beings spend their time in a cycle of birth, life, and rebirth. *Karma* sets the quality of a life according to how well or badly a person lived previously – basically you reap what you sow. The only way out of this endless cycle is to achieve a total knowledge of and union with God.

Sikh spirituality is centred round this need to understand and experience God, eventually becoming one with God. To do this a person must switch the focus of their attention from themselves to God. They get this state of *mukti* (liberation), 'through the grace of God'. God shows people through holy books, and by the examples of saints, the best ways to get close to him. Sikhs believe that God cannot be fully understood by people, but he can be experienced through love, worship, and contemplation, looking for God both inside themselves and in the world around them.

When Sikhs want to experience God, they look both at the created world and into their own souls. Their aim is to see the divine order that God has given to everything, and through it to understand the nature of God. Most human beings cannot experience the true reality of God because they are blinded by their own self-centred pride (*haumain*) and desire for physical things.

The three duties of a Sikh are to pray, work and give. Prayer (*nam japna*) is basically keeping God in mind at all times. Earning an honest living (*kirt karma*) is important; since God is truth a Sikh seeks to live honestly, not just by avoiding crime but by avoiding gambling, begging, or working in the alcohol or tobacco industries. The rejection of a couple of these pursuits puts Sikhs on a cultural clash with much of contemporary Irish life. Finally generosity (*vand chhakna*) is sharing one's earnings with others by giving to charity and caring for others. Sikhs serve God by serving other people and through this they rid themselves of their own ego and pride.

Sikhs try to avoid five vices that make people self-centred, and build barriers against God in their lives. Overcoming these vices is part of the journey to liberation. These vices include lust, greed, attachment to things of this world, anger and pride.

For Sikhs there is only one God, who never takes the form of a human being and is neither male nor female. We know God as he reveals himself and meet God through submission, meditation, the visible world, prayer and living a life of service. Sikhs believe that God is inside every person and so everyone is capable of change.

The main scripture of the Sikhs is the *Guru Granth Sahib*. The tenth and last of the human Gurus, Guru Gobind Singh, declared that nobody would become the eleventh Guru and designated the *Adi Granth* or scripture to be his perpetual successor. Ever since, Sikhs have revered copies of the book as if they were a human Guru. They believe that it guides them through life in the same way as a human Guru.

The *Guru Granth Sahib* contains 1,430 pages with all copies having identical page layouts and numbering. The text is in several languages (mainly Punjabi), but written in the Gurmakhi alphabet throughout. Almost everything in the book is in poem form and intended to be sung, containing the hymns of several Gurus and passages from Muslim and Hindu sources. Despite the great reverence shown to the *Guru Granth Sahib* by Sikhs, they do not worship it since only God is worthy of worship. The reverence to the *Guru Granth Sahib* is not to the book itself, but to the spiritual content, or *shabad*, contained within it. The sacred nature of the *Guru Granth Sahib* means that the sort of textual analysis to which the Bible (for example) is subjected is generally considered inappropriate.

Sikhs are expected to have a place in their home where the *Guru Granth Sahib* can be placed and read. Ideally this should be a separate room, but space limitations often mean that the book sits in a special portion of a room that is only used for 'uplifting' purposes.

Sikhs can pray at any time and any place, although early morning meditation and liturgical payers are close to the norm. Although God is beyond description Sikhs feel able to pray to God as if to a person with whom they have a relationship.

The Gurdwara or 'residence of the Guru' is the temple where Sikhs meet for congregational worship. It is the presence of the *Guru Granth Sahib* that gives the Gurdwara its religious status, so any building containing the book is strictly speaking a Gurdwara. So while the wider population may recognise only two Gurdwaras presently in Ireland, for the Sikh community there are technically dozens. There are no idols, statues, or religious pictures in a Gurdwara, because Sikhs worship only God, and they regard God as having no physical form.

The focus of attention in the main hall of a Gurdwara is the *Guru Granth Sahib*, which is treated with the respect that would be given to a human Guru. The *Guru Granth Sahib* is kept in a room of its own during the night and carried in procession to the main hall of the Gurdwara at the start of the first worship of the day. The book is placed on a raised platform under a canopy and covered with an expensive cloth when not being read. During a service a person will usually fan the *Guru Granth Sahib*.

Four doors lead into a Gurdwara: the Door of Peace, the Door of Livelihood, the Door of Learning and the Door of Grace. These doors are a symbol that people from all four points of the compass are welcome, and that people of all four castes are equally welcome. Shoes are removed and worshippers touch the ground with their forehead.

Sikhs do not have a general order of service to be used in the Gurdwara, although there are rules for particular ceremonies. The morning service begins with the singing of *Asa Di Var*. Other hymns from the *Guru Granth Sahib* are then sung, accompanied by instruments. A sermon or talk, usually based on a theme from Sikh history comes next, followed by the singing of *Anand Sahib*. The congregation then stands with eyes closed facing the *Guru Granth Sahib* for prayer. During the prayer the word *waheguru* (Punjabi for 'praise to the Guru') is often said, having much the same role as the word 'amen' in Christian services. After the prayer, the service ends by opening the *Guru Granth Sahib* to a random page and reading the hymn found at the top of the left-hand page. Food is then normally offered to the congregation. Every Gurdwara has a Langar or kitchen attached to it where simple food is served to anyone without charge. Although Sikhs are not required to be vegetarian, only vegetarian food is served in the gurdwaras.

Sikhs do not have ordained priests, and any Sikh (male or fe-

male) can lead the prayers and recite the scriptures to the congregation. Each Gurdwara has a Granthi or custodian who or-
ganises the daily services and reads from the *Guru Granth Sahib*.

Sikh festivals include those that are associated with the lives
of the Gurus, celebrated with an *akhand path* or complete reading
of Sikh scripture taking 48 hours and finishing on the day of the
festival with the Gurdwara specially decorated for the occasion.
Other festivals include: the birthdays of Guru Nanak and Guru
Gobind Singh, and the martyrdoms of Guru Arjan and Guru
Tegh Bahadur. Vaisakhi or New Year is celebrated on 13 or 14
April, and this also commemorates the founding of the *Khalsa* in
1699. Divali is celebrated by both Sikhs and Hindus.

The majority of Sikh customs are associated with the *Khalsa*,
the body of initiated Sikhs to which most adult Sikhs belong.
Sikhs who have been through the *Amrit* ceremony of initiation
wear the symbols of the five 'K's and take new names; men take
the name Singh meaning lion and women take the name Kaur
meaning princess.

The five 'K's date from the creation of the *Khalsa Panth* by
Guru Gobind Singh in 1699. He introduced them to identify
members of the *Khalsa*, bind the community together and sym-
bolise that the wearer has dedicated himself to a life of devotion
and submission to the Guru.

Kesh or uncut hair, including beard, indicates that one is willing to accept God's gift as God intended it and symbolises adop-
tion of a simple life, the denial of pride in one's appearance and
a symbol of one's wish to move beyond concerns of the body to
attain spiritual maturity. A Sikh should only bow his head to the
Guru and not to a hairdresser. It is a highly visible symbol of
membership of the group and follows the appearance of Guru
Gobind Singh, founder of the *Khalsa*. Sikh women are just as forbidden to cut any body hair.

Kara or steel bracelet is a symbol of restraint and gentility reminding a Sikh that he or she should not do anything of which
the Guru would not approve. It is a symbol of God having no beginning or end, of permanent bonding to the community and of

being a link in the chain of *Khalsa* Sikhs. The *Kara* is made of steel rather than gold or silver as it is not intended to be an ornament.

Kanga or wooden comb symbolises a clean mind and body and the importance of looking after the body that God has created. This does not conflict with the Sikh's aim to move beyond bodily concerns; since the body is one's vehicle for enlightenment one should care for it appropriately.

Kachha is an undergarment that must not come below the knee. It was a particularly useful garment for Sikh warriors of the eighteenth and nineteenth centuries, being very suitable for warfare when riding a horse, although clearly less so today. It is also a symbol of chastity.

Kirpan or ceremonial sword plays an important part in the initiation ceremony into the *Khalsa* when it is used to stir a mixture of sugar and water that the initiate must drink. There is no fixed style of *Kirpan*, and it can be anything from a few inches to a metre long. It is kept in a sheath and can be worn over or under the outside clothing. The *Kirpan* symbolises spirituality, the defence of good and of the weak, the struggle against injustice and is a metaphor for God.

The *Amrit* ceremony is the initiation rite introduced by Guru Gobind Singh when he founded the *Khalsa* in 1699. Sikhs can go through this initiation as soon as they are old enough to understand the commitment that they are making. The ceremony takes place in a Gurdwara, before the *Guru Granth Sahib* and in the presence of five initiated Sikhs. During the ceremony, hymns are recited from the Sikh scripture, prayers are said, and the principles of Sikhism are affirmed. The candidates for initiation drink some *amrit* (a mixture of sugar and water that has been stirred with a double-edged sword) from the same bowl, and have it sprinkled on their eyes and hair. Each then recites the *Mool* mantra (the fundamentals of Sikhism). There are readings from the *Guru Granth Sahib* and an explanation of rules of Sikhism. The ceremony ends with the eating of the ceremonial *karah parshad*.

Adaption and Contribution to Ireland
Visitors to Londonderry on 13 January may be surprised to see bonfires. Not that bonfires are unusual in Londonderry – there are several occasions when the two main communities may light bonfires – but January is restricted to the Sikh community who are celebrating the festival of Lohri.

In common with some other religious communities in Ireland, Irish Sikhs often celebrate their holy days on the Sunday nearest to the festival, accepting that a day when most of the community are free from work is a more pragmatic response to the demands of a particular date that may be a holiday in the Punjab but certainly is not in Ireland.

CHINESE COMMUNITY

Too busy to cook tonight? Chances are the answer will involve a Chinese restaurant given the literally hundreds of outlets throughout the country. Today it is a small village that does not have a Chinese restaurant and Chinese have been Ireland's most significant ethnic minority, beyond the Travelling Community, for half a century. Given their numerical size and relatively long history here, Irish Chinese are starting to make a contribution in many more areas than just catering.

History of the Chinese Community in Ireland
Following the traditional immigration pattern of moving first to Britain and then on to Northern Ireland, Chinese, mainly from Hong Kong, began to arrive in significant numbers in the 1960s. The Chinese catering industry initially flourished, then declined during the severe economic and political problems of the north in the 1980s. This industry has revived and Chinese have diversified into a variety of businesses including supermarkets and hotels. Recent years have seen an influx of Chinese students to Dublin, mainly to learn English. Belfast and Dublin both have a Chinese Chamber of Commerce and there is an Irish-Chinese Cultural Society consisting mostly of Irish people interested in aspects of Chinese culture and life.

WHAT IS THE IRISH CHINESE FAITH?

It could be argued that this section should be dealing with Chinese faiths in the plural, in the same way as Hinduism encompasses a collection of associated religious traditions. Confucianism, Taoism and Buddhism are all part of this Chinese mix. Yet what may be more significance than the distinctive streams of understanding is the Chineseness of these expressions. While China has been exposed to Judaism, Islam, Zoroastrianism and a number of varieties of Christianity, these appear to have remained as foreign religions, with only Buddhism an exception.

Irish people have traditionally belonged to a religious group with a priestly class, true of pre-Christian as much as post-Christian Ireland. In China individuals did not normally associate with an exclusive religious tradition; rather they appropriated religious beliefs to help in different aspects of life. Doctrinal disputes, part of western Christianity as much as in Ireland, do not exist in traditional Chinese belief as doctrinal orthodoxy has never been a feature. Even Buddhism, with a set of core beliefs, found itself changed by this encounter rather than changing Chinese society. In some ways Chinese religion is more a cultural expression than a religion in any traditional sense.

The early Chinese worldview was of a natural world following a cyclical pattern, a pattern of growth and decline understanding the reality of opposites. This view of opposites, or bipolarity, is a specific characteristic of Chinese metaphysics expressed through *yin* and *yang*. Nature existed through the interconnectedness of heat and cold, light and dark, male and female. The *yin* and *yang* are not closed states but rather discernable phases in the constant flow of life.

A belief existed in a Supreme Ruler in Heaven, often written as Heaven, although this concept appears somewhat less than the Judaeo-Christian understanding of God. *Tao* is the way and as such is concerned with ethical and religious truth. It also has a broader understanding of the reality behind or within truth although again is not considered as Deity. Beyond the natural world was an unseen world of spiritual beings; ancestors and those who had been wronged in their earthly life. To protect against the actions of these malevolent beings, a series of charms, firecrackers, mediums, prayers, burning of incense and exorcisms existed to offer protection. All this led to a mysticism based on an understanding of Tao rather than on a Divine Being.

Vietnamese Chinese
The Irish Vietnamese community, originating from approximately two hundred migrants in the late 1970s, is largely ethnically Chinese, many originally speaking Cantonese or Mandarin. The initial group of about fifty settlers in 1975 had been mostly well educated, ethnically Vietnamese, some of whom were Catholic, others being Buddhist or Confucian. Some of this Vietnamese Catholic population had been forced to leave northern Vietnam in 1955 when over 800,000 Catholics moved to southern Vietnam in the final days of French rule. History was again to overtake this community and a generation later they were again on the move.

The majority of Ireland's Vietnamese community are now Irish born and have overcome the disadvantages caused by poor English that hindered many of the first settlers. While a number are university graduates, most continue to be employed in family run Chinese restaurants.

The defining feature of the Vietnamese religious expression in Ireland is ancestor worship. More formally Confucianism, with aspects of Buddhism, is the 'religion' but ancestor worship is how most of the community express their faith. Each home normally has an ancestral shrine, varying in scale and style, but comprising numerous photographs of current and deceased family members, often showing academic, economic or other achievements. A more recognisable religious image will usually be one or more statues of the Buddha, but it is rare that the Buddha will be the dominant image. A second, smaller shrine will usually be found in the kitchen and devoted to the kitchen god or the spirit of the kitchen. This is significant, especially

when it is considered that most of the Irish Vietnamese community find their livelihood in catering, but this shrine is the less
important of the two.

It is the responsibility of the eldest male in the family to
maintain this shrine and flowers and incense are regularly offered before it. Family members regularly gather to pray before
the shrine without a formal liturgy or priests. Even Catholic
Vietnamese will usually have an ancestor shrine although offerings will not normally be made before it.

The significant 'holy days' are the death anniversaries of
family members, clearly meaning there is no Sabbath in any
traditional sense. Family members gather and the male family
head generally leads the ceremony. The house will have been
thoroughly cleaned and fresh flowers, fruit and candles purchased. Traditionally the life history of the ancestor was recited
but migration to Ireland has loosened the ties with and knowledge of the homeland. Joss sticks are lit and shaken before the
alter, food offered before the picture and each family members
individually approaches the image, bows down and prays.
Given the dislocated nature of Vietnamese in Ireland with family
still in Vietnam, it is customary for these rituals to be videoed,
the tape uniting family members across continents in the same
ceremony.

The actual beliefs associated with this form of ancestor worship are hard to define. Two kinds of souls are considered to inhabit humans; *hon*, of which three are present in each person
and *phach* or *via* of which there are seven in males and nine in fe-
males. These souls are related to the forces of nature without an
exact theology being defined. Equally unclear is the destination
of each soul upon death; perhaps a pointer to the centrality of religious practice over religious belief. For the Vietnamese diaspora
the ancestral shrine keeps alive a connection with the home
country and a link to the dispersed family across continents and
generations.

The major festival celebrated by the whole community is Tet
or New Year. On the preceding evening the male head of the

family unites the family by inviting the souls of the dead to join the living, prayer is offered and a party atmosphere ensues as the complete family is together.

In addition to Chinese and Vietnamese who follow traditional Chinese beliefs, there are several ethnic Chinese Christian groups. A Chinese Gospel Church has existed in Dublin for twenty years with its own premises on Middle Abbey Street. This is a very active congregation with a detailed outreach programme to the wider Chinese community. In Belfast the Chinese Christian Fellowship dates back to 1975 and in 1996 had grown to the extent of purchasing their own premises in Lorne Street, Belfast and establishing a more visible presence. These congregations are authentic Irish Chinese expressions of the Christian faith. They have similarities with aspects of a wide variety of Protestant denominations but show a fascinating blend of Irish and Chinese cultural attributes.

The Belfast congregation illustraes a high level of democracy with a Board of Elders elected to guide the church. It is linked to the Chinese Overseas Christian Mission, based in London, which has helped establish Christian congregations among Chinese communities in many British cities. Most of the members of Ireland's Chinese churches are not from a Christian background. They reflect the broad range of Chinese religious understanding but have had a Christian conversion experience.

Adaption and Contribution to Ireland
While there are now third generation Irish Chinese, recent years have witnessed the emergence of racist attacks on this community, mostly, but not exclusively, in Northern Ireland. Ethnic Chinese, with Irish accents, are interviewed in the aftermath of vicious assaults, wondering what has happened to their integration over the previous fifty years.

As ethnic Chinese make an increasingly significant economic contribution to Ireland and are more widely dispersed across the island than any other ethnic group, this recent racist response is especially disconcerting. Hopefully it is not a pointer to a wider malaise in society, one that tolerates difference only when it is constrained within a very small community or within certain geographical boundaries. The Chinese experience, especially in Northern Ireland, of initial relative acceptance that is challenged when economic success and numerical growth create a more vibrant community, is a disturbing one. It may be that it is specific factors, related to the latter days of Northern Ireland's conflict, that has produced this backlash. It is taking the Irish a long time to fully accept diversity, alongside accepting each other.

HUMANISM

Part of a wider movement opposed to traditional religion and promoting free thinking, the Irish Humanist movement, despite its small membership, deserves a mention as a distinct religious expression found in Ireland.

In 1967 a Humanist group was founded in Dublin. It met for around ten years and involved such notables as Justin Keating – a TD and government minister – and Owen Sheehy Skeffington. The group eventually folded as its members became involved in other related issues; Dr Jim Loughran becoming the first chair of the Irish Family Planning Association and Bill and Aine Hyland were influential in the multi-denominational school movement.

The Humanist Association of Ireland was formed in 1993 under the leadership of Dick Spicer, a founder member of the Campaign to Separate Church and State in the 1980s. Members hold ceremonies to name babies, for marriage and death and in 1997 *The Humanist Philosophy: With an Irish Guide to Non-Religious Ceremonies* was published. Major celebrations are Darwin Day on 10 February and World Humanist Day on 21 June. A Northern Ireland group exists and a local group has recently been established in Sligo.

The Humanist Association of Ireland and the Ulster Humanists are part of a major movement but have had little impact in Ireland. While many people may share some aspects of their philosophy, few appear to want to associate with them. In some ways the groups exists as a contradiction. Opposed to the role of organised Christianity in Ireland, the Irish Humanists do not seem to have a similar critique of other organised religions found here. The Christian heritage of Ireland makes this historically appropriate but the developing multi-faith context will show whether the groups are truly humanist or simply anti-Christian.

A second critique is over their 'non-religious' stance. In reality, Irish Humanists have developed their own loose religious understanding. They do not have clergy or a creed but neither do Quakers. The Humanist rites of passage relating to birth, marriage and death are simply a different religious expression rather than a non-religious expression. As this study shows, there are many different rites of passage in modern Ireland and many alternatives to traditional Christianity. Humanists have simply added another variety to Ireland's religious landscape rather than brought the radical alternative they claim.

Some other 'religions' have not been considered. For some groups their statistical insignificance makes their history in Ireland and contribution to the nation very slight – an example might be Zoroastrianism. Other groups are more correctly considered as cults or sects, deviations beyond the bounds of orthodoxy for an existing religion. The wider Irish population may view them as distinct religions but they should be categorised as deviant groups – an example might be Jehovah's Witnesses. Perhaps the only religious group not considered in this work that could argue for inclusion is Satanism or Wicca. This shadowy movement certainly exists and has both adherents, beliefs and practices, a place in national census statistics and those who fulfil the role of clergy. Its lack of visibility excludes it from this study.

CHAPTER EIGHT

Inter-faith Activity in Ireland

Inter-faith activity is not limited to formal meetings between the heads of religions or official representatives. If that were the case Ireland would have virtually no inter-faith history, nor would one be that important. Inter-faith activity does include such events, but the dialogue of life, where one person finds themselves living or working with someone of another faith, is the commonplace inter-faith encounter. In order to make this a real dialogue any differences, real or imagined, in belief, religious practice and social habits are not ignored but rather explored. Dialogue is a place of learning and sharing. Ireland knows a lot about monologue but not so much about dialogue.

The Ecumenical Background

Ireland's recent history has been, to some extent, a history of religious division. The United Irishmen of 1798, joining Protestant, Dissenter and Catholic in a common cause, had given way to increasingly polarised Protestant and Catholic communities. This separation grew until the start of the twentieth century when the northern Protestant community largely aligned itself with Britain and the Catholic community with the cause of a united, independent Ireland. Sometimes forgotten is that during the nineteenth century southern Protestants, such as Parnell, had been among the leaders of the nationalist movement. Yet the generalisation still stands. In nineteenth and twentieth century Ireland religious affiliation was used to help define political allegiance and so helped to highlight significant differences between individuals and between communities. The 1916 Easter Uprising heralded the eventual partition of Ireland in

1922 and hence the current political divisions. The internal divisions between the two main communities in both northern and southern Ireland were as real, if not quite as obvious.

Despite this litany of division based partially on religion, on occasions Ireland has been at the forefront of ecumenical initiatives such as in 1973 when a scheme of union between the Church of Ireland, Methodists and Presbyterians was proposed. 'Towards a United Church' did not receive enough support, especially in Northern Ireland where the very high level of violence was the dominant community issue.

Impetus towards inter-faith involvement has often come from an expanded ecumenical vision that moves from involvement with other Christians to interaction with people of faith beyond Christianity. While the main Irish Protestant churches have committees dealing with ecumenical matters, none currently has a separate committee dealing with inter-faith issues, unlike their British counterparts. More by default than design inter-faith issues are often referred to committees responsible for ecumenical matters.

Currently the Presbyterians are not members of either Churches Together in Britain and Ireland (CTBI) or the World Council of Churches (WCC), although they were founder members of both the WCC and the British Council of Churches, the forerunner to CTBI. However, this lack of ecumenical involvement has not always been the case. In 1906 the Presbyterian and Methodist churches established 'a joint committee for united efforts' and in 1911 a similar joint committee of the Presbyterians and the Church of Ireland was formed. This occurred in an era of great ecumenical initiative centred around the 1910 Edinburgh Missionary Conference, generally acknowledged as the birthplace of the modern ecumenical movement. With added impetus from the 1920 Anglican Lambeth Conference, these two committees developed into the 'United Council of Christian Churches and Religious Communions in Ireland'. In 1966 this name was changed to the 'Irish Council of Churches'.

Pillar of Fire Society

The title of the first Irish inter-faith organisation should go to the 'Pillar of Fire Society'. Previous to this an 'Irish Co-ordinating Committee for the Relief of Christian Refugees from Central Europe' had been established in 1938. Its purpose was self evident from the title and despite the clear Christian emphasis the group included Jewish representation. As a single focus group not directly concerned with discussing dimensions of faith, it should not be considered an inter-faith group in the normal sense but its existence does point to the beginning of formal Christian-Jewish interaction in Ireland.

The Pillar of Fire Society was founded in Dublin in 1942 to enable Jewish-Christian dialogue at a time when news of the mass killings of Jews in Central and Eastern Europe was starting to circulate. While discrimination against Jews had been increasing in Europe throughout the 1930s, few in Ireland believed that a pogrom on the scale of the Holocaust could actually be happening. By 1942 confirmation of the reality and purpose of the concentration camps in central Europe was starting to filter through, even if the full horror was not realised until the Allied victory in 1945. The Pillar of Fire Society was a small but positive part of the Irish response to European events during this period of increasing anti-Semitism.

Composed mostly of Catholic laymen with a smaller representation of Protestants and Jews, the Pillar of Fire Society had only three meetings before it closed due to pressure from Archbishop McQuaid. The principal founder, Frank Duff, who previously had founded the Legion of Mary in 1921, was, in many ways, a strange character to be behind Ireland's first inter-faith body. A career civil servant under both the British and Free State administrations, Duff was briefly secretary to Michael Collins until the latter's assassination. He took early retirement in 1934 when aged forty-five to devote his time to the Legion of Mary. Duff's activities had included strong opposition to Protestant sponsored evangelism in Dublin, especially forms of outreach which he perceived to be taking advantage of the poor and vulnerable and he maintained a very traditional and conservative form of Catholicism. It could be that part of Duff's motivation in helping to found the Pillar of Fire Society was that some Jews might discover the truth of Catholicism. While this evangelistic motivation is usually considered unhelpful in contemporary inter-faith dialogue today, in 1942 the Jewish community responded enthusiastically to Duff's approach, with the Jewish civil servant Laurence Elyan writing to one of Duff's associates, Leon Ó Broin, 'I cannot tell you how delighted I was to get your letter ... I am convinced that we would be doing God's work in promoting a better understanding between our respective co-religionists'.

Duff had a difficult relationship with Archbishop McQuaid and it may have been mainly due to McQuaid's negative attitude to the Legion of Mary that the Pillar of Fire Society indirectly suffered. Duff's relationship in the Dublin Archdiocese is illustrated in that when the Legion of Mary had been in existence for 25 years in 1947 and had been adopted by 550 bishops worldwide, it still had not been officially recognised in Dublin. Two aspects of the Pillar of Fire's meetings were problematic to McQuaid: the expounding of Catholic doctrine by laymen and the issue of Jews lecturing Christians on matters of faith. Under official pressure Ireland's first inter-faith organisation ceased almost as soon as it had begun. The same year, 1942, also marks the date when the Council for Christians and Jews was founded in London, a more enduring group that was later to become a type of successor to the Pillar of Fire in Ireland. A more lasting initiative of Duff's was the opening of the 'Overseas Club' for Afro-Asian students in Dublin, accommodation devoid of racial or religious discrimination where residents of non-Christian faiths were frequently a majority.

Irish Council of Christians and Jews (ICCJ)
The first long lasting inter-faith organisation in Ireland was the ICCJ. Its international background is found in the discrimination of 1920s America where to combat anti-Semitism the

Federal Council of Churches of Christ in America and the Jewish B'nai B'rith organisation set up a 'Committee on Good Will between Jews and Christians'. In 1928 this became the 'National Conference of Christians and Jews', working primarily as a civic organisation promoting joint action among Protestants, Catholics and Jews rather than as an inter-faith organisation.

In Britain the 1924 'Religions of the Empire' Conference prompted the Social Service Committee of the Liberal Jewish synagogues to invite Christians to join with them in a conference in November of that year to consider the role of religion as an educational force. From this the 'Society of Jews and Christians' was formed in 1927, although it should be noted that the 'London Society for the Study of Religions' had included Jewish membership since its inception in 1904. The rise of Nazism in 1930s Germany brought a stream of refugees to Britain prompting Christian attempts to understand the Jewish religious context in addition to responding to the physical needs of these refugees. Under the patronage of the Anglican Archbishop William Temple, the 'Council of Christians and Jews' was formed in 1942 to combat intolerance and foster Jewish-Christian co-operation with Revd Bill Simpson, a Methodist minister, serving as secretary for the first thirty-two years. The first joint Presidents included William Temple, Cardinal Hennesey, the Chief Rabbi Dr Hertz and the Moderators of the Church of Scotland and the Free Church Federal Council.

Post war Oxford, 1946 was the setting for the first gathering of the American, British and other national groups, from a total of fifteen countries. Participants included the noted author Alan Paton who represented the South African Society of Christians and Jews which was to be closed by the South African government in 1948. In 1962 the International Council for Christians and Jews was founded which, by 2002, included thirty-six national committees. In the last few years the movement has considered more seriously the relationship between the three Abrahamic faiths.

During the 1970s there was a growing engagement between

the Christian community and the Jewish population in Dublin. Christian groups would visit Adelaide Road Synagogue to learn of their Jewish heritage and this developed into regular discussions and Christian-Jewish parties held alternatively in a convent school and synagogue. With this groundwork helping to promote understanding the ICCJ was established in June 1981, largely as an initiative of the Sisters of Zion, to promote understanding and mutual respect between Christians and Jews and to highlight the common roots and values they share. Under the patronage of the Chief Rabbi and leaders of the Roman Catholic, Anglican, Methodist, Presbyterian and Lutheran communities, the council currently meets every four to six weeks to explore common areas of interest shared between the faiths and to arrange public lectures and seminars. The Council has sponsored the award of the 'International Council of Christians and Jews' Gold Medallion for Inter-Faith Work' to President Robinson in 1996 and President McAleese in 2003 and helps to organise other 'one-off' events such as Holocaust Memorial Day, acting as a body to co-ordinate events involving both Jews and Christians. Given the decline in Irish Jewish numbers over the past 40 years, the future direction of this group is unclear.

The Council of Christians and Jews (NI) was founded in February 1996, with the support of the Belfast Jewish Rabbi Revd Eli Kohn, Cardinal Daly (Roman Catholic), Bishops Poyntz and McMullan (Anglican), and Methodist and Presbyterian representatives. The speaker at the opening public meeting was Lord Coggan, the former Archbishop of Canterbury. The Co-Chairmen were Canon Houston McKelvey and Revd Eli Koh with Dawn Quigley as Honorary Secretary. In 2003 the Presidents were Archbishop Sean Brady, Archbishop Robin Eames, Revd Prof John McCullough and Revd Dr Johnston McMaster, representing each of the four mainstream Christian traditions. The normal programme consists of approximately six public lectures per year and, since 2002, an annual Holocaust memorial event. The Dublin and Belfast branches usually try to hold an annual joint meeting.

Just why the Belfast branch was formed in 1996 is open to question. The Jewish community at the time of the Council's formation numbered around 300, mostly elderly and with no immediate likelihood of this decline being halted. Further, the Northern Ireland Inter-Faith Forum had been in existence for five years by this time, a body seeking to represent all religious communities in Northern Ireland. Finally there was the significant growth of the Belfast Muslim community, currently much more numerous than the Belfast Jewish population. The wisdom of a Christian inter-faith initiative directed at a declining religious minority while, at the same time, largely ignoring a significantly growing religious community is debatable. Part of the answer may have been the desire to engage with the Jewish community while there still was a Jewish community. In another generation the opportunity may have gone.

The Northern Ireland Inter-Faith Forum (NIIFF)
The first significant world inter-faith gathering was the World's Parliament of Religions in 1893, and this was to have a direct link in the formation of the NIIFF one hundred years later. In 1890 the US Congress decided that there should be a 'World Exposition' in Chicago in 1892 to celebrate the arrival of Christopher Columbus in 1492. Practical reasons meant it was not until 1893 that the Exposition took place, with cultural events designed to show to Europe a sophisticated and mature USA.

Charles Bonney, a lawyer and educationalist, advocated that the Exposition should contain a congress of world statesmen, scientists and teachers. This idea was developed by the organising committee into a series of twenty distinct congresses, including religion, with Bonney as the overall chairman. A committee to oversee the religion congress was established with Roman Catholic and mainstream Protestant figures prominent, but which also included Dr E. G. Hirsch, a Reform Rabbi. In an attempt to make the event truly inter-faith, 3000 copies of the preliminary address were sent in June 1891 to religious leaders across the world to explain the purpose of the congress and elicit support. Early supporters included Max Muller, a scholar in the developing comparative religion discipline, although there was far from universal support, with William Gladstone and the Sultan of Turkey among those opposed to the meeting. The USA Presbyterian Assembly of 1892 voted against participation while E. W. Benson, Archbishop of Canterbury, was also opposed due to his refusal to attend an event where non-Christians could comment upon the Christian faith. Roman Catholic dignitaries participated throughout the conference but without fully endorsing the event. In 1895 Pope Leo XIII officially censured Catholic involvement in any similar event. Bishop John Keane of the Catholic University of Chicago, who had enthusiastically supported the Parliament, was dismissed from his academic position in 1896.

At 10am on 11 September 1893 representatives of twelve religions processed though a 4000 strong audience to begin the parliament. The Christian influence, indeed dominance was obvious from the beginning of proceedings as the 100th Psalm was sung and Cardinal Gibbon of Chicago led the delegates in the Lord's Prayer. Of the 194 papers delivered 78% were by Christians, the majority of whom were North American Protestants. Bonney's opening address stressed the commonality of religion. Those responding included P. C. Mozoomdar (Hindu), Pung Kwang Yu (Chinese), Rt Revd Reuchi Shibata (Shinto) and H Dharmapala (Buddhist). One of the 'stars' of the parliament was the Bombay Hindu reformer Swami Vivekananda whose opening words 'sisters and brothers of America' were greeted by a prolonged burst of applause and who has been described as 'the most important figure of the 1893 parliament'. Only one Muslim spoke at the conference, Muhammad Alexander Russell Webb, a western convert. Followers of Jainism, Confucianism and Zoroastrianism were present and while no Bahá'i attended, the faith was referred to.

The Parliament lasted for sixteen days with each day devoted to a single theme including 'systems of religion', 'God', 'Sacred

Books' and 'the religious of the whole Christian family'. Two specifically Christian themes were 'the present religious condition of Christendom' and 'the religious reunion of Christendom', highlighting the Christian bias. Various Christian denominations used the opportunity to meet on their own, surely a divisive note in an inclusive gathering. Perhaps the greatest strength of this Parliament was the friendships made across religious divides. Receptions were held in the evenings to facilitate this but it was often casual encounters that opened the way for greater religious understanding.

The Parliament was a dramatic, if not fully realised, statement of a coming plural world. Christians had originated the conference, held the central, even dominant position, but acknowledged that they were not alone. Some western voices had accepted Christianity as one religion among many. Some eastern voices, coming from a context of long established but proportionally very small Christian churches, had challenged the normal western assumptions of the supremacy of Christianity.

In 1896 a Christian-Buddhist conference known as the 'Little Parliament of Religions' was held, but it was very much smaller in both scope and impact than its predecessor. The direct successor to the 1893 Parliament dates from 1988 when two Hindu monks from the Vivekananda Vedanta suggested organising a centenary celebration. In 1993 8,000 people from around the world gathered in Chicago, producing the Hans Küng inspired document 'Towards a Global Ethic: An Initial Declaration'. Speakers included Robert Muller of the United Nations, Harvey Cox and the Dalai Lama. Four Jewish groups withdrew at the last moment when an invitation was issued to Louis Farrakhan of the 'Nation of Islam'. The Greek Orthodox Diocese of Chicago refused to participate, citing the impossibility of dialogue with some who did not believe in God.

To make this movement more permanent a continuation council was established which has developed small-scale projects but which has also initiated a regular series of Parliaments meeting roughly every five years. The Irish Nobel Peace Prize

recipient Mairéad Corrigan-Maguire currently sits on the
International Advisory Committee. Cape Town, December 1999,
witnessed approximately 7,000 participants from eighty countries. The document, *A Call to Our Guiding Institutions*, was issued to challenge many of the world's most powerful institutions to reflect on their role for a new millennium. Barcelona in
July 2004 was the venue for the latest Parliament.

Given this background, and 1993 designated as 'a year of
inter-religious understanding and co-operation' to celebrate the
centenary of Chicago 1893, the NIIFF was formed in May 1993
with the aim of promoting friendship and mutual understanding across the variety of Ulster's religious spectrum. Other factors leading to the formation of the NIIFF included encouragement from the ICC, the involvement of educationalists and of
those who could be described as 'interested individuals'.

The Revd Maurice Ryan, a Presbyterian minister and lecturer
in Stranmillis College, Belfast was the chief instigator of the
NIIFF and without his personal initiative the group would not
have been formed by 1993. Prior to this, for educational reasons
related to Northern Ireland's Educational for Mutual
Understanding programme as well as personal interest, Ryan
had established contacts with various faith communities in
Northern Ireland and produced *Small World: A Handbook on
Introducing World Religions in the Primary School* in 1988, the first
publication of its kind in Ireland. Also in 1988 Ryan met with Dr
David Stevens of the ICC, during a period when the various
non-Christian religious groups in Northern Ireland had no formal or significant contact with each other, apart from the small
initiatives of the Columbanus Community. Dr Stevens encouraged Ryan's inter-faith initiatives although this ICC role was
fairly minimal, perhaps what could be described as tacit support. Yet it was still significant and helps illustrate the involvement of ecumenical Christians in inter-faith activity in Ireland.
This is not remarkable – it would be more surprising if
Christians who were not willing to associate with other
Christians, with whom they had differences in understanding,

were then willing to meet with non-Christians to discuss issues concerning their respective faiths.

Ryan was encouraged by representatives of the various religious communities to continue his initiative. Practicalities were discussed with the UK Inter-Faith Network and eventually a small group representing the Christian, Jewish, Hindu, Muslim, Buddhist, Sikh and Bahá'i communities was established in Belfast. This group has never become numerically significant and in May 1999 the Forum had 98 members who were recorded as Jewish 6, Hindu 10, Muslim 9, Buddhist 7, Bahá'i 9, Sikh 1, Roman Catholic 14, Presbyterian 11, Anglican 13, Methodist 7 and others 11. Despite a small membership it has initiated a considerable number of projects and become the leading voice of inter-faith activity in Northern Ireland. Membership is in an individual capacity with only the Non-Subscribing Presbyterian Church of Ireland officially appointing a representative. Meetings for members are usually held around four times a year at Stranmillis College, Belfast, with occasional public meetings held on specific issues. The NIIFF explains its purpose as 'to promote friendship and mutual understanding across the spectrum of religious and ethnic life in Northern Ireland, and to encourage charitable purposes for the community as a whole'.

The main initiatives have been as follows:

1. An international conference in Armagh on 26-27 February 1998, co-hosted with the International Inter-Faith Centre, Oxford and attended by Archbishops Eames and Brady.

2. 'At Home with People of Other Faiths', an initiative to create informal contacts between people of differing religions.

3. Establishing the 'Quiet Room' at Belfast International Airport as an inter-faith place of prayer, opened on 24 February, 2000.

4. Hosting a visit by the Dalai Lama in October 2000.

5 Hosting a 'Multi-faith Celebration of Peace' in St Anne's Cathedral in October 2000. This was perhaps the first occasion in Northern Ireland where representatives of various religions had publicly participated in inter-faith worship.

6. The Religious Diversity Training Programme, a major government sponsored initiative.

7. 'In Good Faith' travelling exhibition, in conjunction with Diversity 21, the Community Relations Council and the BBC, describing the different faith communities of Northern Ireland.

8. Meetings with government officials to discuss inter-faith issues.

9. Participation in Holocaust Day events in co-operation with Belfast City Council and the Belfast Jewish community.

10. Publications including *Another Ireland* by Maurice Ryan, *A Tapestry of Beliefs* by Norman Richardson, *Welcome! An Introduction to the Faith Communities in Northern Ireland, Check Up! A guide to the special needs of hospital patients from Northern Ireland's ethnic-religious minority communities*, and occasional 'Inter-Faith Calendars' for Northern Ireland.

From this survey of NIIFF activity a number of observations can be made. The NIIFF is a collection of interested people and not a meeting of official representatives of religious groups. This makes for a harmonious gathering but must limit the wider impact of the group. A body such as the ICC has delegates appointed to it by various churches and these delegates can speak and act officially on behalf of their denomination. However, while members of the NIIFF may hold official office in their faith community, they meet in the NIIFF as individuals. A corresponding group in this regard could be the Evangelical Alliance (Northern Ireland) whose membership is either personal or corporate (a local congregation or Christian organisation). While the Evangelical Alliance can only speak on behalf of its members and not on behalf of 'evangelical denominations', it has a significant voice due to the large number of personal members.

A related question is over the designation of 'Forum'. In many British cities, with Leicester a notable example, there is an inter-faith council where representatives of various faiths meet. These councils can act in significant ways to overcome religious problems in the wider community and to reflect general religious opinions to government and other bodies. The NIIFF cannot do this and although the other faith communities in Northern Ireland are much smaller than those in most British cities, these communities have still the same social, economic, racial and political challenges as in Britain. Due to its nature the NIFFF may not be able to address these community issues and in the future an inter-faith council may need to be formed. Such a group could well emerge out of the NIIFF or else could be formed independent of the Forum and possibly make the NIIFF irrelevant to the wider community.

There is a question as to why the Forum is operating only in Northern Ireland and not on an all Ireland basis. The combined non-Christian population of Northern Ireland and the Republic of Ireland is statistically still very small and these communities face many of the same issues in both jurisdictions. Geographically Ireland is a fairly small country with good infra-structure between the cities making distance only a small consid-eration. Despite the two political entities there are many exam-ples of cross border bodies and sporting teams, rugby and hockey being notable examples. More relevantly, almost all Christian de-nominations are organised on an all Ireland basis. Of course the historic Christian denominations were in existence before parti-tion but even post 1922 most denominations consider Ireland to be a single religious entity. The ICC is an all Ireland body, al-though the Evangelical Alliance is restricted to Northern Ireland with a sister organisation recently established in the Republic of Ireland, and the Council of Christians and Jews has separate branches in Belfast and Dublin. Arguably inter-faith issues in Ireland could be better served by having a body representative of the whole island constituted in a similar way to the ICC.

The impact of the NIIFF on the wider community is minimal. In a personal survey of Christian denominations in Northern Ireland, of nine responses received four had not even heard of the body and none had much specific information. Perhaps this is not surprising due to the Forum's small membership, absence of full time staff and limited scope of work, but it is still an indi-cation of a lack of impact in the community.

The emphasis on education is arguably both a strength and a weakness. Two of the founders, Maurice Ryan and Norman Richardson, are academics at Stranmillis College while many other members, if not working full time in education, still had an educational dimension to their work. The publications of the NIIFF have been mostly educational, for use in schools or by students, while others assist health workers in dealing appropriately with patients from minority faith communities. In this area the Forum has been very successful, supplying the materials and expertise necessary for the educational and health services in Northern Ireland, receiving government support, financial and otherwise, for this. Production of educational material that helps promote awareness of religious diversity within the private and public sector is currently being undertaken. This will take the educational dimension of the NIIFF out of the school sector into the workplace and long term could significantly raise public awareness of the Forum. While general educational work could be considered the major area of success, yet this is also a weakness in that the Forum may be viewed as largely an educational resource with little other relevance. Some inter-church groups, such as the Columbanus Community, concentrated on identifying with minority faith communities, especially the Jewish community, by attending their worship and social events. This does not seem to happen in the NIIFF. Rather members come together to work on a document or discuss a topic and then leave, with the respective communities unaffected. To make a province-wide impact the NIIFF surely needs to expand its area of interest beyond education to other community issues.

The Three Faiths Forum of Ireland (TFF)

On 3 March 1999 the Lord Mayor of Dublin, Councillor Senator Joe Doyle, formally launched the Three Faiths Forum of Ireland at a function in the Mansion House where speakers included Sr Carmel Niland, Imam Yahya Hussein, Chief Rabbi Gavin Broder and Canon Des Sinnamon. The Forum had been meeting regularly since September 1997, discussing areas of faith and the

need for education to break down prejudices and misunderstanding, prior to the launch in 1999.

The impetus for the group came from two main sources with
the more significant being an initiative of the Irish Council of
Christians and Jews. In the early 1990s Ireland's Muslim population was growing and the ICCJ considered it appropriate to initiate discussions with this community to form a body that could
engage people of all three Abrahamic religions. Sr Carmel
Niland made approaches to the Muslim community and, after
initial Muslim reluctance, a preliminary meeting was held in
September 1997, out of which an embryonic Three Faiths Forum
was founded. In doing this the ICCJ was following the lead of
the British Council of Christians and Jews who have helped to
develop 'Abrahamic' or 'Three Faith' groups, looking to the
common Abrahamic inheritance as a starting point, although
this has not happened in Northern Ireland.

The second source was the initiative of Canon Des
Sinnamon. In the 1980s he was the Church of Ireland Rector of St
Catherine and St James on Dublin's South Circular Road which
had a synagogue and the first Irish mosque as near neighbours.
Initial contacts between his parish and the growing Muslim
community were largely on the social level of welcome but relationships were built. Later Sinnamon moved to Taney Parish in
south Dublin and in the mid 1990s he found some unease among
parishioners concerning the building of the impressive Irish
Islamic Centre at Clonskeagh. In order to diffuse any tensions
among his parishioners Sinnamon made contacts with the leadership of the new mosque and initial meetings, allied with the
initiative of the ICCJ, helped to develop into the Three Faiths
Forum. Other individuals had called for a similar group including Patrick Comerford, then Foreign Desk editor of the *Irish
Times* and currently head of the Anglican Church Missionary
Society in Dublin.

Based in Taney Parish Centre, Dublin, the TFF holds regular
public meetings, issues statements on behalf of its constituents
and has the following aims:

1. To bring together representatives of the three Abrahamic faiths in Ireland – Jewish, Christian and Muslim – for regular meetings, to create a Forum for religious dialogue between faiths, thereby strengthening relations and increasing mutual understanding.
2. To promote education, to provide accurate information about the three faiths, and to involve a wider public in the dialogue in order to build a better society.
3. To encourage individuals and groups to come to know one another better, to break down prejudice and misunderstanding and to work both separately and together for tolerance, goodwill, respect and co-operation.
4. To take common action when there is discernment that issues of justice and peace are at stake.

The effective working of the TFF is illustrated in the meeting on 1 April 2003 between Cardinal Connell and Noah Al-Kadoo, Director of the Islamic Cultural Centre of Ireland. This meeting was arranged to discuss respective attitudes to the then ongoing war in Iraq and issue a joint statement, helping to minimise any potential Irish anti-Iraqi feeling that may be directed at the Muslim community. The meeting was facilitated by Fr Brendan Leahy, the official Roman Catholic Diocesan representative to the TFF, and provided quick access for one religious leader to another.

There are a number of obvious differences between this body and the NIIFF. Firstly, the membership of the TFF is by appointment from the individual religions and Christian denominations represented. Secondly, the TFF does not seek affiliation with any outside bodies whereas the NIIFF is a member of the Inter Faith Network of the United Kingdom. Thirdly, the TFF is seeking to start similar groups in other Irish cities while the NIIFF has no such plans. The Belfast based group views itself as representing Northern Ireland, although it must be noted that the title of Three Faiths Forum of Ireland is not particularly appropriate if the intention of that body is only to serve Dublin.

Arguably the TFF will make a greater long-term impact than the NIIFF although currently the opposite seems the case. Official representation on the Dublin body allows it to speak for all three communities in a way the Belfast group cannot. After the 11 September 2001 terrorist attack on New York and Washington, the statement of the NIIFF was that of a group of concerned individuals, whereas the statement from the TFF was that of three faith communities.

Yet the Dublin body has a significant problem; while it represents communities it only represents some of Ireland's faith communities. There are more Buddhist centres than mosques in the Republic of Ireland and a Sikh Gurdawara has been present in Dublin for over twenty years. Hindus, Bahá'is, Buddhists and Sikhs are not represented on the TFF and, as these communities grow, the need for an 'Inter-Faith Council' representing all religions in Ireland becomes more urgent. When, and surely it is only a matter of time, such a body is formed the TFF is in danger of being sidelined. To some extent this could have already happened with the establishment in March 2003 of the Immigrant Council of Ireland, chaired by Sr Stanislaus Kennedy. Yet it could be that the TFF will be the group to initiate such a religiously inclusive body, although there are currently no plans in this direction. The reason cited is the TFF's need to become established among those that share the Abrahamic inheritance before official relationships are developed with further different religious groups. It could be that the TFF will become a subgroup of a wider based Inter-Faith Council. This would appear to be a useful development although similar TFF's have developed out of Councils of Christians and Jews but not gone on to widen their base. Most TFF's in UK have developed after the establishment of inter-faith councils.

There are two major world inter-faith movements that have had a small impact in Ireland.

World Thanksgiving
This movement began in 1961 with the desire of the City

Planning Council in Dallas, USA to have a city centre area to celebrate a 'value'. Eventually in 1976 a garden and chapel in
Dallas were opened, followed by a Hall of Thanksgiving the following year, close to the site where John F Kennedy was assassinated. An annual Thanksgiving Declaration signed by twelve religious leaders was first issued in 1982 and seminars are regularly
held, speakers including Robert Runcie, the Dalai Lama and
John Templeton. In 1994 the organisation started an annual programme to explore the theme of thanksgiving in the major
world religions.

After visiting the square in Dallas, Myrtle Smyth proposed
building a 'Thanksgiving Square' in Belfast. She first raised this
idea at the Ophsal Commission in 1992 and by 1999 a one third
acre site in central Belfast beside the river Lagan was given for
this project. The then Secretary of State for Northern Ireland, Dr
Mo Mowlan remarked, 'Northern Ireland has known much pain
and suffering. Now we are at the beginning of a new era of peace
and prosperity. The creation of this place of thanksgiving is
symbolic of a better tomorrow for us all.'

This initiative has even allowed the tiny inter-faith move-
ment in Northern Ireland to be noticed in the British Parliament.
On 9 February 2000 Revd Martin Smyth, then Official Unionist
MP for South Belfast, raised the matter of the funding of the
square. He asked the Parliamentary Under-Secretary of State for
Northern Ireland (George Howarth), 'Does the Minister accept
that Thanksgiving Square – proposed by Jews, Muslims,
Hindus, Christians and others – would be useful in finishing the
Waterfront?' The reply was positive. It could be that this small
initiative will be the first major inter-faith symbol in Ireland. The
Dallas Square is used for regular inter-faith events; such happenings would be an interesting addition to the religious make
up of Northern Ireland.

The International Association for Religious Freedom (IARF)
One of the world's major inter-faith organisations with Non
Government Organisation (NGO) status at the United Nations,

the IARF has had Irish involvement from its inception. The Non Subscribing Presbyterian Church of Ireland (NSPCI) was a founder member of the IARF and members of that church have regularly participated in international IARF events. In 1955 the fifteenth IARF Congress was held in Belfast on the theme of 'Liberal Religion in an Age of Anxiety' with the meetings taking place in various NSPCI premises. The Congress was favourably covered by the press; the *Belfast Telegraph* reported on 30 July 1955 that, 'It is good to have clear and enlightened views, but it is still better to show that such beliefs possess a moral dynamic, and can make men lead strong, courageous, and helpful lives.'

A Northern Ireland branch was formed in 1996, although it has been largely inactive since 2001. Currently there is a local membership of approximately thirty, almost all Non-Subscribing Presbyterians with Revd David Steers as chairman and Sandra Gilpin as secretary. Steers is a Non-Subscribing Presbyterian minister and currently serves on the IARF International Committee. While the IARF could have made a significant impact in the religiously divided Northern Ireland context, its local, largely mono-denominational Christian membership has meant its influence has been limited to this one small community.

Ecumenical Bodies with an Inter-Faith Involvement
One of the responses to the divisions in Northern Irish society has been the formation of a number of ecumenical groups that have considered reconciliation between the communities as their calling. A number of these have developed a level of inter-faith involvement and it is to be expected that this will expand in future years as inter-faith matters become more significant, both for the world and for Ireland. An example of this is St Clement's Renewal and Reconciliation Centre on the Antrim Road, Belfast. On 18 June 2003 the community hosted a British 'Peace Council' visit to Belfast where leaders from Buddhist, Muslim and Christian communities shared their respective understandings of peace. While this inter-faith involvement has not been a significant part of St Clement's ministry and there are currently no

plans for future inter-faith initiatives, if the pattern of the groups considered below is followed, then St Clement's Centre will gradually become more involved in inter-faith work, as a consequence of their ecumenical vision.

Corrymeela

Established in 1964 under the leadership of Revd Ray Davey, Corrymeela has become an internationally recognised centre for reconciliation. Begun with a clear Christian impetus, the Christian ethos of the work has remained constant, with community member Ian Gilchrist writing in *Corrymeela Connections* in 2000 that, 'Corrymeela remains centred on Christ'. Yet inter-faith awareness was present from the beginning and has become a small, but growing, part of the Corrymeela work.

Long before the centre was established, Davey had helped to establish a wartime centre in Tobruk to be used by all faiths in chaplaincy to soldiers. Pastor Tullio Vinay, founder of the Agape reconciliation centre in Italy, provided much of the early inspiration to Davey and others and he performed the opening ceremony for the Corrymeela building. In 1983 Vinay was awarded 'The Medal of the Just' by the Israeli government for saving the lives of Italian Jews during World War II. Issues of the various Corrymeela magazines contain references to inter-faith work such as stressing Robin Boyd's participation in inter-faith dialogues. Boyd was ordained an Irish Presbyterian minister who served in North India for many years before transferring to the Uniting Church of Australia. Later he was Director of the Irish School of Ecumenics from 1980-1987.

In *Occasional Paper No 2*, Dr William Rutherford, a community member and medical doctor, compared the inter-church work of Corrymeela to a wider inter-faith understanding and argued how the former often leads to the latter. Rutherford was a Presbyterian missionary in India for a number of years and became an influential surgeon in the Royal Victoria Hospital, Belfast, dealing with the consequences of Northern Ireland's violence. He wrote:

But in interchurch or interfaith dialogue one discovers that others too have deep and cherished convictions. And as the dialogue proceeds neither one's own position nor that of one's opponent remain as directly conflicting as it first appeared.

In May 1986 the Revd Inderjit Bhogal, a long-term supporter of Corrymeela and future British Methodist President, who was raised as a Sikh and became a Christian as a young adult, brought a Wolverhampton inter-faith group to the Corrymeela centre.

Arguably the inter-faith interest of Corrymeela has increased in recent years. In 1997 Corrymeela was awarded the Niwano Peace Prize by the Niwano Foundation of Japan and in March 2000 Corrymeela welcomed a group of eighteen volunteers from Rissho Kosei-kai, a Japanese lay Buddhist Organisation associated with the Niwano Foundation. This organisation had chosen Corrymeela to be a recipient of their annual distribution of 'Dream Bags' containing gifts from Japanese children to under-privileged children. Perhaps the significant aspect of this visit for this study was the inter-faith celebration that was part of it. Inter-faith worship appears to be an area in which Corrymeela is increasingly confident enough to engage in.

At Belfast's 'The Way of Peace' seminar in November 2000 the then Corrymeela community leader, Revd Trevor Williams, was asked to chair what was arguably Northern Ireland's most significant inter-faith event due to the participation of the Dalai Lama, although the Armagh 1998 conference had a much wider religious representation. A conference considering the insights of non-Christian faiths in relation to reconciliation, forgiveness and peace was held in June 2002. In April 2003 a significant inter-faith conference was held at Corrymeela in conjunction with the International Interfaith Centre in Oxford. Participants gathered to consider 'Religion, Community and Conflict: Youth Initiatives for Peace' and finished with an interfaith worship service. While inter-faith work is not central to Corrymeela's vision, it does appear to be playing an increasing role.

The Columbanus Community of Reconciliation (CCR)

The Columbanus Community was inaugurated on 23 November 1983 under the leadership of Fr Michael Hurley SJ as an ecumenical community whose members would have paid employment outside of the group. Part of the idea for the community had come to Fr Hurley in the multi-faith city of Calcutta while on a sabbatical in February 1981. The first resident community consisted of four Catholics, one Anglican and one Presbyterian and was based on Belfast's Antrim Road, a mixed Catholic-Protestant part of the city that had already witnessed a very significant amount of violence by the early eighties and which would continue to suffer in this way during the life of the community. Columbanus sought to be a witness to reconciliation within a divided city.

The inter-faith aspect of Columbanus was present from the inauguration in 1983 but happened largely by accident. North Belfast was chosen as the location of Columbanus due to its Catholic-Protestant mixed population, but that area was also home to many of Belfast's Jews and to the city's synagogue. A Jewish representative was invited to the community opening and almost every week a member of the community attended the Saturday synagogue service. While the main work of Columbanus was in attempting to reconcile Protestants and Catholics and inter-faith involvement was never a major focus, there were Jewish/Christian contacts from the beginning. Later inter-faith encounters developed with Buddhists, Bahá'i, and Sikhs among others. Beyond synagogue attendance, daily interaction with Jewish neighbours was seen as an important aspect of community life. Community member Eileen Lyddon became housekeeper to Rabbi Granewitz and the Christian-Jewish interaction was seen as a symbol of reconciliation between two communities who shared the history of the holocaust.

A survey of the *Columbanus Newsletters* reveals that out of thirty-five editions covering almost twenty years, inter-faith involvement was mentioned in twenty-four editions, this at a time when the Irish Christian denominations were making virtually no reference to inter-faith issues. While inter-faith work may not have been a founding principle of Columbanus, the community showed a long-term commitment to this form of reconciliation.

Over the years Columbanus organised other inter-faith events including lectures on the Jewish community in Belfast, talks by followers of other faiths, and the facilitation of visits from individuals from various faith backgrounds. Encouragement was given to the formation of the Northern Ireland Inter-Faith Forum and the Council of Christians and Jews, with a member spending a sabbatical in India to explore avenues for future inter-faith encounter. They initiated a small local inter-faith group of Christians and Hare Krishna devotees, the executive of the CCJ (NI) met in the Columbanus house and a Buddhist monk lived with the community for six weeks. Yet there were limits to this engagement. A local Buddhist community wished to use the Columbanus house for regular worship and did so for a short while but there was opposition from some CCR members and the Buddhist group's permission was terminated. This opposition may have had more to do with what supporters and donors of Columbanus might have thought over the 'promotion' of Buddhist worship rather than the views of community members, highlighting the fact that Columbanus was a Christian group interested in inter-faith encounter rather than an inter-faith group.

One issue that emerges from the Columbanus inter-faith experience is the question of Christians worshipping with people of non-Christian faith. The community never invited any non-Christians to lead their community prayers. Hurley considered that the community members, as individuals, could worship God in the context of the Jewish synagogue but that they were not participating in the Jewish worship in the same way as the Jewish believers and so this activity could not be classified as inter-faith worship. Despite this view, in 1999 Columbanus hosted an event they described as an 'interfaith service' with a team of Christians, Muslims and Buddhists who built a 'peace garden' at Columbanus. This team had originally intended to work with Habitat for Humanity in Belfast but that invitation was withdrawn when the team connection with Revd Sung Myung Moon and the Unification Church was realised. On completion of the garden a 'Bridge of Hope' ceremony was held involving all the participants.

The exact approach of Columbanus towards other faiths during its period as a residential community is hard to determine, partially due to the principle that Columbanus supported member involvement in various outside activities not directed by Columbanus. It was always an association of people living in a community but working as individuals outside of that community. What does emerge is a picture of a community who sought to implement its aims by including others in its Christian life of prayer, reflection, work and recreation, while reaching out to those of other faiths. Columbanus made a significant contribution to inter-faith understanding in Belfast and gave a lead to other groups that were to follow with a more specific focus.

The Cornerstone Community

Similar to Columbanus, the Cornerstone Community was founded in 1982 to promote reconciliation between Catholics and Protestants in west Belfast. It consists of a small residential community with associated non-residents, all sharing the vision of reconciliation. There has been a small inter-faith involvement with Revd Sam Burch, Fr Gerry Reynolds and Geraldine Connolly of the community involved with the CCJ (NI). Cross-cultural links have been a feature of Cornerstone involving local Indian and Chinese communities, but religion has played only a small part in these meetings. The former Director of Cornerstone, Tom Hannon, is a member of the NIIFF and has had personal links with the local Bahá'i and Buddhist communities.

Cornerstone's inter-faith involvement is less significant than that of Columbanus, but is still of note in an era of little inter-faith activity. Again it is those involved in ecumenical work who are involved in this inter-faith work. It could be that in a Northern Ireland context there is a significant 'leap of faith' required to move out of the narrow denominational community and the wider Catholic-Protestant division into ecumenical contact. Once that bridge has been crossed an inter-faith step is not so difficult to take. There appear to be very few Christians involved in inter-faith activity who are not also involved in ecumenical work.

The Glencree Centre for Reconciliation (GCR)

The GCR is a one hundred member-based association seeking to promote tolerance, respect and greater understanding between individuals and groups in conflict situations. Started in 1972 and based in Enniskerry, Co Wicklow, the organisation seeks to reflect the changing political, cultural, societal and religious environment of Ireland. GCR was founded with a Christian basis which later broadened to include those who wished to be involved in reconciliation but could not subscribe to the original Christian emphasis. It has engaged in a number of religiously based programmes seeking to foster reconciliation in Ireland, recognising the religious dimension to the ongoing conflict.

In some ways the GCR is a Republic of Ireland equivalent to Corrymeela, engaging in much the same areas of work, although Corrymeela operates from an explicitly Christian basis. Reflecting the increasingly plural profile of Ireland, Glencree has developed a relationship to the Muslim community through connections with the Islamic Cultural Centre in Clonskeagh, Dublin and through diplomatic contacts in the Islamic world. It is to be expected that the inter-faith dimension of the GCR's work will increase in the future, due to the changing nature of the Irish population but also to the increasing awareness that insights from other religions may be beneficial in seeking to decrease conflict in a post Christian society.

Irish School of Ecumenics (ISE)

Formally inaugurated on 9 November 1970, the ISE developed through the initiative of Fr Michael Hurley SJ. Hurley's initial vision was exclusively inter-church with no mention of 'Inter-

faith Relations' or 'Peace Studies', the other two strands of the
ISE programme that were to develop. It was not until 1978 that
the inter-faith dimension began, being seen as an outworking of
ecumenism. The contemporary student body occasionally includes Muslim, Jewish or other faith students.

As the ISE developed, inter-faith dialogue was introduced to
the curriculum and courses offered currently include 'World
Christianity and Interreligious Dialogue', 'Judaism and Jewish-
Christian Relations', the 'Islam and Muslim-Christian Relations',
and 'Issues in Buddhist-Christian Dialogue'. In Northern Ireland,
the ISE has embarked on a series of courses and seminars seeking to bring the perspectives of world religions into the context
of Northern Irish social ethics. The significant 1998 inter-faith
conference held in Armagh was partially arranged by the ISE.

John D'Arcy May is currently Fellow and Associate Professor
for Interfaith Dialogue at Trinity College Dublin, a unique appointment in Ireland, and it is he who provides much of the ISE
impetus in the inter-faith area. An Australian Roman Catholic,
May received his doctorate in History of Religions from the
University of Frankfurt in 1983. He worked as Ecumenical
Research Officer with the Melanesian Council of Churches and
was visiting professor in Fribourg, Switzerland (1982), Frankfurt
am Main, Germany (1988) and Wollongong, Australia (1994).
May has written widely, most recently authoring *After Pluralism:
Towards an Interreligious Ethic*. May's work applies a critique to
the optimism of Hans Küng's 'global ethic' and the pessimism of
Samuel Huntington's 'clash of civilisations'. He reminds us of
those who are often forgotten in the world of inter-faith discourse: women, followers of indigenous religion and those in
poverty; those he calls 'the feminine, the primal and the poor'.
This reminder is even more important in Ireland than in some
other countries as these three voices are still marginalised in our
context where the majority of participants in formal faith discussions are male, middle class clergy who generally have little
knowledge or contact with other faith communities.

Recent guest lecturers at the ISE have included inter-faith

scholars such as Paul Knitter and the ISE is arguably the only Irish body that actively promotes inter-faith dialogue beyond the parochial confines of Dublin and Belfast. The international dimension of the student body, faculty and visiting lecturers opens Ireland to the influences of inter-faith thinking from a number of other contexts. The Irish history of dominant Christianity in two mono-ethnic states is very different to most world regions and by exposing students and others to wider themes the school helps to create a more balanced understanding of the inter-faith encounter. If inter-faith dialogue is only seen in the context of an overwhelming Christian majority then it can be perceived as a Christian exercise in charity and inclusiveness. When it is viewed in situations where Christians are numerically and economically much weaker, the dialogue takes on a different dimension. That is part of what the ISE brings to the Irish inter-faith scene.

In November 1995 the ISE sponsored Ireland's first major inter-faith conference, inviting eminent academics from across the world but also including representatives of the various Irish faith communities. Speakers included Wesley Ariarajah, Paul Knitter, Gavin D'Costa and Ursula King and the papers were published as *Pluralism and the Religions: The Theological and Political Dimensions*. Conferences of this kind expose Irish students and others to a range of radical thinking and scholarship that is normally absent from Ireland, while the location enables eminent practitioners to engage in critical reflection within the Irish context. A creative dynamic ensues that can significantly advance Irish thinking and provide a stimulus for further study and action. Arguably the ISE is the only Irish body capable of organising such an event. A comparable event was the inter-faith conference held in Armagh in 2000, but it could be viewed as an inter-faith event that happened to be held in Ireland but which did not specifically engage in the Irish context.

The Royal College of Surgeons in Ireland (RCSI)
The RCSI was the first institution to attract significant numbers

of Muslim students to Ireland from the 1950s onwards, with a number remaining to work and helping to create the present Irish Muslim population. In its early years a number of Irish Jews also studied at the RCSI; today the college has a very significant percentage of Muslim students and its own Mosque. Occasional inter-faith events are held in the RCSI, reflecting the religious makeup of the students. Inter-faith worship can take place in the context of 'An Inter-Faith Service of Thanksgiving and Remembrance' for those who have donated their bodies to the cause of medical education and research in the College.

The only officially appointed chaplain currently at RCSI is Rev William McLaren, a Church of Scotland minister. The issue of non-Christian chaplains is something that Irish colleges have been slow to consider. Queen's University, Belfast (QUB) has Muslim and Jewish chaplains, but no other Irish university currently has appointed non-Christian chaplains. QUB does not financially support its chaplains and so there is no financial implication in having Muslim and Jewish chaplains. In Trinity College Dublin there is a Muslim prayer room and also a Jewish 'community student chaplain' although he does not have any official university status, nor does he receive the same support as the Christian chaplains. In University College Dublin there is no recognition of other faith chaplains, although provision of prayer rooms and the close proximity to the Clonskeagh mosque does assist that particular faith community. None of the other Irish universities currently recognise non-Christian chaplains. This question will need to be addressed in the near future.

Other Inter-Faith Initiatives
There have been a small number of other inter-faith initiatives. It is to be expected that in future years there will be more such initiatives; hopefully some future initiatives will come from non-Christians as inter-faith work in Ireland has largely been initiated by Christians to date.

The Sisters of Zion

Based in Bellinter, Co Meath, the Sisters of Zion were established in Ireland in 1965 with the specific aim of promoting a greater understanding between the Church and the Jewish people, and a deeper respect between all races, traditions and minorities. While the Sisters of Zion have become involved in other reconciliation, educational and Christian work, this inter-faith aim remains their main focus.

Two French Jewish brothers, Alphonse and Theodore Ratisbonne, who both converted to Christianity and became Roman Catholic priests, founded the order in 1843. Their intention was not to mount a crusade seeking the conversion of other Jews but rather to explore more fully the Jewish roots of Christianity and bring a better understanding between the Jewish and Christian communities. Starting in a small way, the congregation is now found in twenty-three countries, played a significant role during World War II and made contributions to the discussions that resulted in *Nostra Aetate*, the significant Vatican II document that helped redefine Catholic inter-faith understanding.

In Ireland the Sisters of Zion are involved in organising retreats considering the Jewish aspects of Christianity, in promoting dialogue between the Christian and Jewish communities and in teaching on Jewish and inter-faith issues at second and third level colleges. They support groups such as the ICCJ and the TFF. Sr Maura Clune was the first leader of the community in Ireland, and was succeeded by Sr Carmel Niland, currently secretary of the ICCJ. The Sisters of Zion also lead a Women's Inter-Faith/Inter-Cultural Group which meets occasionally in Dublin and holds a 'Celebration of Culture' day at Bellinter each June.

The Jewish response to the Sisters of Zion was always been polite but in the first fifteen years little progress was made in fostering deeper relationships, partially due to the negative Jewish experience of Christian evangelism. The arrival of Rabbi Rosen was a significant factor in improving contact between the communities and, together with Sr Niland, he participated in the ISE Jewish-Christian Relations course. Rabbi David Rosen served as President of the International Council of Christians and Jews. The Order maintains a valuable role in facilitating communication between the Jewish and Christian communities.

Harmony

The 'single focus' group Harmony was established in Dublin in 1986 to promote understanding among people of all backgrounds in Ireland and to campaign for the introduction of comprehensive anti-racism legislation. It had a short but effective life as anti-racist legislation is now in place in both jurisdictions. While not specifically an inter-faith group, inter-faith was an important aspect as many of the racial minorities in Ireland have non-Christian majorities. However, it is worth noting that the most significant minority racial group traditionally present in Ireland, the Traveller Community, is almost exclusively Catholic. Many of the new immigrants to Ireland are also from Christian backgrounds including many of the eastern Europeans, many Africans and the Portuguese community in Northern Ireland.

Regular meetings were held and papers published to highlight the anti-racist agenda. More secular groups such as the 'Anti Racism Campaign', 'Immigrant Solidarity' and 'Residents Against Racism' have taken on this work in the Irish Republic. In Northern Ireland organisations carrying on this agenda include the 'Committee on the Administration of Justice', the 'Northern Ireland Council for Ethnic Minorities', the 'Northern Ireland Council for Ethnic Equality', and the 'Northern Ireland Community Relations Council'.

Cardinal Connell's Regular Meetings

Seemingly in imitation of Pope John Paul II's inter-faith prayer initiative at Assisi, Dublin's Cardinal Connell occasionally invited religious leaders from Dublin to meet together to pray for peace. Entitled 'Religions Gathering for Peace', the 2002 meeting involved participants reading together a 'Common Commitment to Peace' where the prominent voices were those of Archbishop Empey (Anglican), Imam Ali Al Salah (Muslim) and Cardinal Connell (Roman Catholic). The smaller Christian denominations and other religious groups responded together and this approach reasonably accurately reflected the numerical importance of the communities represented. Each religion then met separately for prayers so that there was no inter-faith worship as such, following the same pattern as the gathering at Assisi.

This event shows the increasing opportunities for leaders from various religious groups to meet together. In praying for peace an important aspect of each faith is acknowledged as a truth that is held in common. Praying for peace is something that people of faith do, whatever that faith may be. As a gesture, this initiative by Cardinal Connell pointed to a growing recognition that the Archdiocese of Dublin is a multi-faith environment and respect is given to all communities. While a small gesture, it contributes to making a pluralist, inclusive society where people of various religions are welcomed and affirmed. It is expected that Archbishop Martin, who succeeded Cardinal Connell in April 2004, will continue these initiatives. In his various Vatican appointments Martin has had interaction with numerous international and inter-faith bodies and is a founding trustee of World Faiths Development Dialogue.

Conclusion

Ireland's inter-faith organisations are relatively new and sometimes short lived, as in the case of the Pillar of Fire Society or Harmony (Ireland). They exist alongside related groups that are not specifically inter-faith in focus, such as the various ecumenical or educational bodies mentioned. The NIIFF and the TFF, both of recent origin, are the first truly representative inter-faith bodies to emerge in Ireland. The ICCJ and the CCJ(NI) are clearly inter-faith but their limitation to just two faiths disqualifies them from being fully inter-faith. Possibly the inter-faith credentials of the TFF could be challenged on the same criteria. While the three faiths included in its membership cover the vast majority

of Irish population, other faith groups are excluded. This leaves
the NIIFF as arguably the only fully inclusive inter-faith group,
a poor record, especially as earlier chapters have highlighted the
many hundreds of years of Irish inter-faith experience.

As the minority faith communities grow it is to be expected
that the NIIFF and the TFF will increase in size and significance.
If not, other groups will probably emerge to fulfil needed functions in a more secular way; perhaps in a more community-
based way in Northern Ireland or in a more inclusive way in the
Irish Republic, bearing in mind the perceived weaknesses of the
NIIFF and the TFF.

Ecumenical groups, such as Columbanus, have played a
prophetic role in pointing to the need for inter-faith engagement. Their ecumenical focus has meant that inter-faith activity
has been, at best, a part-time preoccupation, and at worst a dis-
traction from their main work. Their lack of significant success
in inter-faith work is not unexpected given this limitation but
they have highlighted the need for others to take up this task.

It has also been noted that inter-faith initiatives have been exclusively Christian in orientation. This is not surprising given
the overwhelming numerical, political and economic strength of
the Christian community. However the increasing organisation
of the other faith communities, especially the Muslims, gives the
potential to address this imbalance.

While Ireland's inter-faith history is relatively brief and recent, the range of groups involved and the level of activity
reached so far is worthy of note. That Ireland's future will involve more inter-faith activity, both formal and informal, goes
without saying. Just how quickly this will develop and what impact this will make on Ireland in the future depends on what
happens in the present.

CHAPTER NINE

Towards a Better Ireland

It is a great country that cannot improve. When Harold Macmillan was telling the British population in the 1950s that they had never had it so good, there was still much room for improvement. Even Bono of U2 admits that he still hasn't found what he's looking for. Ireland still has a long way to go. The historic Protestant/Roman Catholic division that has scarred Ireland for too many generations is beyond the scope of this work. A relationship between politics and religion is not unique to Ireland although the rest of Europe appears to have largely overcome negative aspects of the Reformation legacy. Perhaps what is relevant here is that the divisive nature of this interaction has largely disappeared in the Republic of Ireland in the past generation. The early Protestant involvement in Ireland was normally backed by political and military force and post independent Ireland, at least beyond Dublin, became a cold place for Protestants. Small Protestant communities were eroded by migration and inter-marriage, while many Protestants closer to the border moved the few miles further. The independence war in the south and subsequent IRA campaigns targeting border communities are a terrible part of this history. The phrase 'ethnic cleansing' may have come to prominence in the Balkans during the 1990s but the practice was apparent in twentieth century Ireland directed against portions of the Protestant community. Of course, rereading earlier Irish history shows ethnic cleansing by English authorities to create small Protestant enclaves in the first place, and the early 1970s witnessed micro scale ethnic cleansing on the streets of Belfast, even if families only moved a hundred yards. A search back into Irish history rediscovers successions of such atrocities, whether by Celts, Vikings, Normans, English or those we call Irish. History is written by the victors but is also rewritten by politicians, freedom fighters and just about anyone who wants to justify their present actions. Given Ireland's literary tradition, let us not be surprised that we are more adept at this than most.

All that said, Ireland has changed and is still changing. The two confessional states of the 1950s are consigned to memory and almost folklore. Churches no longer dominate society, although their influence is still significant. The boycott of the Protestant community at Fethard on Sea is only fifty years ago, yet it seems like another age, which indeed it is. Catholic Ireland is gone and with it the old certainties and divisions, replaced by a new pluralism that brings its own challenges. Of course, in areas close to the border with Northern Ireland this reality may not be so obvious but overall, for the Republic of Ireland at least, there is a developing experience. All this means that acrimonious religious division is not a necessary element of Irish society, nor is it inevitable. That it still remains, especially in a sectarian nature in Northern Ireland, is lamentable but change is possible. Today Orangemen roll up their trouser legs and paddle in the sea on the annual walk at Rossnowlagh. Portadown's Garvaghy Road no longer witnesses the naked hatred of the turn of the millennium, but nor does it example two communities for whom the past is history. While Protestant Ulster has gone, its replacement has not yet been determined.

Taking the change in Catholic-Protestant relations in the Republic of Ireland as a precedent, the relatively recent establishment of significant non-Christian faith communities in Ireland need not raise any level of religious animosity. We need to learn, and then keep to the fore, the fact that Irish contacts with these faith communities stretch back far into the past, often for more than one thousand years. That these communities are innocent of bringing religious animosity into Ireland is clear. Any religious discrimination members of these communities might suffer is fully the responsibility of Ireland's nominally

Christian community. The more recent faith communities have been the passive recipients of Irish welcome, apathy and hostility. The host community has always been the active partner.

It is also not acceptable to argue that the arrival of people from abroad has been responsible for a rise in religious or ethnic discrimination and so the simple solution to this 'problem' is to remove the cause i.e. the presence of those that are 'other'. If we took that approach, Ireland would have been depopulated centuries ago. The arrival of people who might follow a different religion or customs is not a problem. If some react negatively to their presence, this reaction becomes a problem. The negativity needs to be addressed, not the presence in Ireland of Muslims, Hindus, Buddhists, Jews and whoever. As we have seen, the Irish population is composed of historic waves of migrants. A small number of attacks on eastern Europeans resident in Ireland illustrates that such responses are not motivated primarily by religious or ethnic hatred. A Lithuanian is likely to be as Christian and as ethnically similar to the cosmopolitan mixture that is defined as Irish. The negative response by a few, and thankfully it is only a very few, is directed to those who are the 'other'. It might have many different motivations, none of which are acceptable or even coherent. But Ireland is not 'in trouble' because of the recent establishment of new faith communities.

Ireland's embryonic multi-faith context is not just a situation where a host Christian population engages, to a greater or lesser extent, with newcomers. Fifth generation Irish Jews might be a little confused by such a generalisation, as would third generation followers of Chinese religion. Muslim school children in Ireland are increasingly likely to talk with Irish accents. These Irish have a responsibility to play their part as much as anyone else. One of the disappointing factors to emerge from this study is the lack of contact between the newer religious groups. Beyond the official inter-faith bodies, whose limited impact has already been discussed, there is, for example, no significant relationship between Ireland's Jewish and Muslim communities. In the 1980s Nick Harris recorded the following inter-faith 'incident':

I remember that the Muslims who were coming to Ireland at that time offered to buy the Greenville Hall Synagogue. The figure mentioned was around a quarter of a million pounds, but Rev Gittleson would not hear of it. They wanted to convert the synagogue to a mosque. When Rev Gittleson died suddenly a year or so later, the synagogue was sold for much less than the Muslims had offered.

That blame for less than perfect inter-faith relations can be shared among all faith communities is of little comfort, nor does it point to a better future. Apportioning blame is an Irish pasttime that various tribunals on both sides of the border have allowed to develop into an industry that, while making lawyers and others very wealthy, does little to heal the hurts. A 'Truth and Reconciliation Commission', akin to that of South Africa, has been mooted for Northern Ireland but never seriously contemplated. A similar body to deal with child abuse scandals in the Republic of Ireland has proved problematic, although the state has limited the compensation payable by the Catholic Church, partially in an attempt to encourage full disclosure of past crimes to enable the healing process for those physically and emotionally damaged. Attempting to blame the smaller faith communities for any inter-faith misunderstanding or coldness does not move Ireland forward.

Yet there has been some surprising progress in what, on the surface, seems less than fertile inter-faith soil. The staunchly politically Protestant support for Linfield, one of Northern Ireland's most successful soccer teams, historically has found it difficult, although not impossible, to accept team members from an Irish Catholic background. The sectarian nature of football support in Glasgow mirrors this on a larger scale. Yet the arrival of some North African players in the 1980s brought a challenging interfaith context. How would these staunch political Protestants cope with Muslims playing for their team? How did this fit into the 'us' and 'them' context of Belfast soccer support? Well, basically they were warmly welcomed and accepted. Whatever they were, they were not Irish Catholics. Similar examples could be given from Glasgow Rangers and Glasgow Celtic. Herein lies part of the inter-faith hope for Ireland. Newcomers do not neatly fit into Irish sectarianism. If they are seen as not 'them' so therefore 'us', then this gives hope for a better inter-faith future. Hindus, Muslims and Buddhists are not hostages to Irish history in the way Protestants and Catholics still appear to be. It remains to be seen whether many of the Africans who have recently come to Ireland, a significant number of whom are active Christians, will become embroiled in this Irish form of tribalism.

Yet, in Northern Ireland, the sectarian captivity of society appears to be winning. Some newcomers are being viewed as 'not us' so therefore 'them', widening the divisions in society. My personal hope is that this is a temporary expression and the presence of Hindus, Muslims and Buddhists will help decrease Northern Ireland's tensions. As numbers increase, there will be a gradual diffusion of difference in local areas. The boundaries of small, localised mono-cultural communities will become blurred, state schools will include Muslims alongside Protestants, Catholics schools will educate Hindus and the sharp distinctions become blunted. Not everyone will welcome this dilution. Traditions and social cohesion are important, but too often localised Irish communities gained their identity by proclaiming what they were not rather than what they were. This has lessened in recent years, but is still a factor in cultural expression. As the Gaelic Athletic Association has liberalised itself in recent years to allow members of Northern Ireland and Britain's security forces to join, and allow other sports to use Croke Park in Dublin, it was noticeable that the impetus for such inclusive actions did not come from the northern counties. Orange Lodges are becoming more interested in expressing the cultural rather than political nature of their organisation, but talking to certain community groups somehow seems a step too far.

All that said, the virtually complete healing of Protestant and Catholic antagonism in the Republic of Ireland, at least away from the border counties, has shown there can be a better future.

Ireland need not repeat past attitudes in the future. Government actions, particularly in the Republic of Ireland, have promoted pluralism and broadly welcomed change. So, if we are to avoid replicating in the inter-faith context the sectarian nature of much of Ireland's past and part of her present, how do we get there? Let me suggest five principles that may be part of the journey.

1. Look to the heart of each faith, not the extreme edges

A basic principle of inter-faith encounter is to listen to what is being said and accept that view, rather than project your own, possibly inaccurate, preconception onto your colleague in the encounter, be they a neighbour, workmate, relative or official representative of their religion. The actions of the Taliban in their short control of Afghanistan are fairly irrelevant to a meeting between Christians and Muslims in Portadown or Dublin. The Christian partner in the meeting will not appreciate or find it relevant to be reminded and quizzed about the actions of the Spanish Inquisition, Crusader knights or Cromwell in Drogheda. Not that any of these events should be expunged from memory or record; they exist and do affect relationships, but express an excess and distortion of Christianity and Islam rather than the heart or ideal. Islam at its best and Christianity at its best should be the initial points of contact. As dialogue and friendship develop, there is opportunity to face up to difficult issues and historical legacy, but simply characterising Christianity as justifying apartheid and Islam as justifying suicide bombers is inaccurate and unfair to both religions.

This is a difficult lesson for Ireland to learn. We are fond of dredging up historical events to be used in an attempt to bolster our own position by discrediting the 'other'. Happenings of three or four hundred years ago still have life in Ireland. Let us avoid adding the crusades and the Indian 'mutiny' to the list that most of us know only too well.

Ireland has known a few extreme expressions of Christianity in the past and present. It has not experienced extreme Islam or Hinduism. It could well be that the followers of these various world faiths in Ireland are more moderate within their wider religious community than many of Ireland's Christians.

The extreme edges of a religion are just that, extreme. They are populated by relatively few, although they might be very vocal and carry out actions that bring prominence to their perspective. Sometimes it is necessary to recapture the middle ground, not in a desire to water down the essentials of a faith to make it more acceptable to others, but to reaffirm the heart of a religion. Being extreme does not make an individual more pious or religious than a moderate contemporary. It often simply means that the extreme follower has a distorted understanding of his or her own faith. Occupying the centre ground has been an uncomfortable place in Northern Ireland. It takes courage and conviction, something that can be learnt from Ireland's non-Christian communities.

2. Do onto others as you would want them to do onto you
Irish Christians want to be welcomed, accepted and given the freedom to worship wherever they go. In contemporary Ireland it is occasionally proving difficult for followers of Islam, Hinduism, Sikhism and other faiths to establish places of worship. Most of these populations live in cities where land is scarce and costs high. Economics and demographics are against them. Christian churches have been quick to share their premises with ethnic Christian congregations who have come to Ireland. Often language will be a significant factor and so various Protestant and Catholic churches host ethnically Nigerian, Romanian, French speaking etc congregations. The Chinese churches are the historic example of this. Even major denominations like the Russian or Romanian Orthodox have been assisted in this way.

What about Hindus, Buddhists and Muslims? Muslims worship in a former Presbyterian church building in Dublin and Hindus in a former Methodist hall in Belfast, but no church has opened its premises to a non-Christian worshipping community, apart from the Salvation Army allowing Muslims the use of a room for a prayer room in Dublin in the 1950s. This is not that surprising. Christian churches are what they say they are – Christian churches. Whatever their inter-faith understanding it would still be surprising for any to allow their worship centres to be used for non-Christian worship. Church buildings apart, Christian owned halls that act as community centres could be viewed differently. They might be owned and managed, for example, by the Roman Catholic Church or Church of Ireland, but are not generally used for Christian worship. Rather they are used for a variety of Christian related activities and by various community and sporting groups that do not have a particular religious perspective, even if many members come from a particular religious tradition. Could these premises be offered to non-Christian faith communities for their worship as they establish themselves? This offer would not be on the level of equating, say, Hindu worship with Christian worship but on the level of neighbours helping each other. It is commonplace for Protestant congregations to meet in another's premises when their own is being repaired or built. In the Republic of Ireland it is becoming common for this to cross the Protestant-Catholic boundary. Can one more boundary be crossed? Time will tell, but this is one example of treating others the way Irish Christians would wish to be treated.

If sharing church premises with others for worship is problematic, perhaps what is easier for Christians to do is to stand up for the rights of religious minorities. Ireland has learnt the lessons of the recent past and generally Christians no longer discriminate against those of other Christian traditions. So does this extend to supporting the right of minority religious groups to have freedom of worship and freedom to propagate their faith? These are both considered basic human rights under the United Nations charter. Recent events in Craigavon, where the Muslim community has faced opposition to their plans for Northern Ireland's first purpose built mosque, suggest some are not willing to extend full human rights to this community. The Protestant community in particular have a tradition of claiming civil and religious freedom, of protecting their freedom of worship and insisting on their rights to evangelise, even when not particularly welcome in a specific location. These rights are appropriate for a faith community but need to be given to all. It should be Christians who are active in insisting on the rights of the Muslim community to be able to establish suitable places of worship. There may be very good practical reasons why a particular location does not satisfy planning permission but Christian voices should be heard promoting the cause.

On the level of evangelism it should be Christians who support the rights of other missionary religions, such as Islam and to a lesser extent Buddhism, to evangelise in Ireland. Irish Christians rightly maintain the appropriateness of spreading their message with others and this is a right that needs protecting. A pluralist society that sees no place for the propagation of a particular religious perspective should not be welcomed by Christians. When Muslims stand on the street corner and preach, when Buddhist literature is pushed through letter boxes, when Hare Krishna devotees hold open air worship, some of the other Irish are not so pleased. Yet these groups are simply doing what Irish Christians, and especially evangelical Protestants in recent generations, maintain as a part of their faith. The right to spread a particular religious understanding in appropriate ways needs to be maintained for all in contemporary Ireland.

3. We must want a better future than our past

Some look back to the 1950s, north and south, as a golden era of religious adherence and societal cohesion. Some, but not many. Discrimination was rife in both jurisdictions and where a religious community has a virtually unchallenged position, abuses of personal and corporate power too often result. Neither economy was particularly robust and migration was a national curse. There were, of course, many positive aspects to community life in that and previous eras but my point here is that it was not as good as it could be. Can the future be better than the past? It is debateable whether contemporary Ireland is an improvement on the past. Economically Ireland, especially the Republic of

Ireland, has dramatically improved and the peace process in Northern Ireland continues to hold the line between animosity and sectarian violence. Crime appears to be increasing, morality in a traditional sense is certainly decreasing. Whatever your perspective on where Ireland was in the past and is today, all can still desire a better future.

Ireland has a developing religious context that brings new possibilities. This can be embraced as a positive experience that can benefit Ireland in ways previously unimaginable. Our cultural creativity is being enriched by a multitude of new perspectives and outlooks. Our sporting teams are gaining the prowess of many national backgrounds. Our economic capabilities are being bolstered by the best of the world drawn to a wealthy and vibrant Ireland. Our religious expression is being multiplied.

In her own strength and against many obstacles, Ireland has come a long way and established herself as a significant European nation with a diaspora to bolster her position in the world. Today Ireland can start to draw on resources beyond what she traditionally had. Instead of some of the best and brightest of Ireland being forced by economics or politics to migrate, Ireland is now retaining her own and being supplemented by the brightest and best from a multitude of nations. Now, before I get carried away, not everyone who comes to Ireland is guaranteed to be an outstanding economic or cultural addition to the nation; even the most optimistic Irish voice will concede that not every Irish migrant brought only blessing to their new land. That was not the case for those that left and it will be the same with those that come. Yet the point is still valid. Ireland is stronger today than she was before because of newcomers. Let us celebrate that and enjoy the benefits.

It is obviously possible to see new religious communities as a problem. Ireland no longer is only a Christian country; we are no longer all the same, although were we ever? Instead of crosses and churches, we start to come across mosques and statues of the Buddha. For some this is difficult to accept. Christian Ireland is in the past and the future seems strange and uncertain. When we travel to exotic destinations on holiday some want to experience everything they can about the new culture; its food, language, climate, history, religion. Others want Irish weather, to speak English and eat only clearly recognisable food. That is human nature; we are not all the same. Part of living in the twenty first century is increasing diversity. The world has shrunk and Ireland has been drawn into the mainstream rather than remaining a relatively backward nation on the periphery of Europe. One of the consequences of this movement has been the recent establishment of some faith communities. Not everyone will embrace this. It is a learning curve for most. But it is the present and increasingly the future.

4. Let us use the new opportunity that Ireland's contemporary inter-religious context provides as an example to the world
Ireland has an enviable position regarding interreligious issues when compared to most of the rest of the world. Because Ireland did not have a colonial empire, there are no nations harbouring bitter memories of cultural and religious oppression. The crusades passed Ireland by with barely a mention, absolving us of one negative aspect of the current western-Muslim context. Of European countries with Jewish populations in the twentieth century, Ireland has an exemplary record. Our cities do not have large, economically deprived, ethnic ghettos. This all means that history has given Ireland a surprisingly advantageous interfaith position. This has been supported by current government policies in the Republic of Ireland to promote pluralism and very little contemporary Islamaphobia or anti-Semitic activity.

Given all this, Ireland has the opportunity to show the rest of the world what a plural, integrated multi-faith nation can be. This is not to say that such nations do not exist. Of course they do, but many countries with long established good multi-faith contexts are exhibiting signs of stress; examples range from India to Holland to Australia.

Ireland can be an experiment as to how progressive government policies, building on a positive past, can create an integrated, plural country. As with all experiments the outcome is not certain. That we have a long way to go is stating the obvious, but the possibility is real. Ireland's inter-faith future is not yet determined but the opportunity to positively affect it currently exists. In another ten, or certainly twenty years, patterns of behaviour and societal responses will be hardened and Ireland will either be the example of good practice, or be another lost opportunity. Now is the time to build the future.

5. Teach the stories of the past to the present and future generations
Ireland has an inter-faith past and, as this study has shown, it is largely a positive experience. Men and women who worship in a mosque or temple, synagogue or gurdwara are not strangers or visitors but new Irish from particular faith communities with whom the Irish nation has had a relationship going back over many centuries. This needs to be understood. Policy makers need to know our historic relationship to better inform the present. Teachers need to realise that religion classes in Irish schools have an important, good story to tell. Social and community workers need to recognise the contribution to Irish society of the differently Irish over many generations. Church leaders have to accept that the religious leadership of Ireland is no longer only Christian. And most importantly we can embrace what it means to be Irish, in the breadth of that statement.

There are many other lessons to be learned over the next few years. Some of these are in micro issues. For example, national censuses still record the membership of fairly obscure Christian denominations but ignore distinctions within Islam or Judaism. Perhaps the answer to this question will be for the state to recognise the irrelevance of counting differences within particular faith communities. The broader issues of inclusion, consensus building, promotion of religious freedom and freedom of worship and anti-racism are before us. The particular focus of this work has been to highlight the inter-faith context of past and present Ireland. The future inter-faith relationship is in our hands. Ireland, north and south, can be an example to the world of an integrated society. This is not a pipe dream. Over the past fifty years the Republic of Ireland has moved markedly from a state where Protestants 'kept their heads down' to one where allegiance to a particular Christian denomination is largely unimportant. My personal desire is not to see a time where an individual's religious understanding or particular faith community is irrelevant. Rather it is to be part of a nation where religion is a personal expression of who you are and not an inherited label of what you are not. Religion becomes something that is fundamentally spiritual and not a description of what part of a town you might live in, who you might vote for or what team you will cheer on at the weekend. As Hindus, Buddhists and Muslims do not neatly fit into the mould of Ireland, the hope is that they will help us break this mould with its inherent restrictions.

Being Irish opens doors around the world. People like the Irish; we are sociable, warm, cultured and only fight with ourselves. As the world has, and still does, embrace us, let us fully embrace the Muslim, Hindu, Buddhist and Jewish Irish in the expanding expression of what it means to be Irish. Not because it is the politically correct thing to do, but because this study has shown that Ireland is already composed of religious migrants and we are simply doing what, to a greater or lesser extent, has made Ireland what it is today. Together we are stronger, and tomorrow can be better than today – if we fully accept the challenge.

Appendix 1

Northern Ireland Census

	1991	*2001*
Islam	972	1943
Hindu	742	825
Judaism	410	365
Bahá'i	319	254
Buddhism	270	219
Humanism	69	40

Source: Northern Ireland Census 2001

Republic of Ireland Census

	1991	*2002*
Islam	3900	19147
Hinduism	953	3099
Judaism	1581	1790
Bahá'i		490
Buddhism	986	3894

Source: www.cso.ie

Appendix 2

Contact details of Irish Faith Communities

Bahá'i

> Irish Bahá'i Centre
> 24 Burlington Road, Dublin 4
> www.bahai.ie

> Bahá'i Council for Northern Ireland,
> Hackney House, 64, Old Dundonald Road,
> Belfast, BT16 1XS
> e-mail bcni@bahai.org.uk

Buddhist

> The Buddhist Centre
> 56 Inchicore Rd, Kilmainham, Dublin 8
> www.buddhism.ie

> Dublin Buddhist Centre
> 42 Lower Leeson Street, Dublin 2
> www.dublinbuddhistcentre.org

> Dublin Shambhala Meditation Group
> 19 Herbert Street, Dublin 2
> www.dublin.shambhala.ie

> Jampa Lang Tibetan Buddhist Centre
> Co Cavan
> www.jampaling.org

> Rigpa Ireland
> 12 Wicklow Street, Dublin 2
> www.rigpa.ie

Tara Buddhist Centre
18 Long Lane, Dublin 8
www.meditateireland.com

Tashi Khyil Tibetan Buddhist Centre
54 Derryboye Road, Crossgar, Co Down BT30 9LJ

Chinese

Chinese Gospel Church
49 Middle Abbey Street
Dublin 1

Chinese Christian Fellowship
Belfast

Hindu

Hindu Temple and Cultural Centre
Carlisle Circus, Belfast

Dublin Hindu Community
www.ivt.ie

Belfast Hare Krishna Temple
140 Upper Dunmurry Lane, Belfast BT17 0HE

Hare Krishna Island
Innis Rath, Derrylin, Co Fermanagh

Dublin Hare Krishna Community
Govinda's Restaurant
Aungier Street,
Dublin 1

Humanist

Humanist Association of Ireland
www.irish-humanists.org

Ulster Humanists
www.nireland.humanists.net

Jewish

Office of the Chief Rabbi
Dublin 6
www.jewishireland.org

Belfast Synagogue
The Wolfson Centre, 49 Somerton Road,
Belfast

Terenure Hebrew Congregation
Rathfarnham Road, Dublin 6

Machzikei Hadass
Terenure Road North, Dublin 6

Dublin Jewish Progressive Synagogue
Knesset Orach Chayim, 7 Leicester Avenue, Dublin 6

Irish Jewish Museum
Walworth Road, Portabello, Dublin 8

Cork Hebrew Congregation
South Terrace, Cork

Stratford Schools
Rathgar, Dublin 6

Muslim

Islamic Cultural Centre
19 Roebuck Road, Clonskeagh, Dublin 14

Islamic Foundation of Ireland
163 South Circular Road, Dublin 8

Muslim National School
Roebuck Road, Clonskeagh, Dublin 14

Belfast Mosque and Community Centre
38 Wellington Park, Belfast
www.belfastislamiccentre.org.uk

Sikh

Sikh Cultural Centre
1 Simpson's Brae, Londonderry

Dublin Gurdwara
78 Serpentine Avenue, Merrion Road,
Ballsbridge, Dublin 4

Select Bibliography

Ali, T., *The Clash of Fundamentalisms*, London: Verso, 2002

Allen, R., *Arnold Frank of Hamburg*, London: James Clarke, 1966

Armstrong, K., *The Battle for God: Fundamentalism in Judaism, Christianity and Islam*, London: Harper Collins, 2001

Bartlett, T. & Jeffrey, K. (eds), *A Military History of Ireland*, Cambridge: Cambridge University Press, 1996

Bewley, C., *Memoirs of a Wild Goose*, Dublin: Lilliput, 1989

Bourke, A., *The Burning of Bridget Cleary: A True Story*, London: Pimlico, 1999

Bradshaw, B. & Keogh, D. (eds), *Christianity in Ireland: Revisiting the Story*, Blackrock: Columba Press, 2002

Brown, D., *A New Introduction to Islam*, Oxford: Blackwell, 2004

Braybrooke, M., *Pilgrimage of Hope*, New York: Crossroads, 1992

Cahill, T., *How the Irish Saved Civilisation*, London: Hodder and Stoughton, 1995.

Carew, M., *Tara and the Ark of the Covenant*, Dublin: The Royal Irish Academy, 2003

Chambers, A., *Ranji: Maharajah of Connemara*, Dublin: Wolfhound Press, 2002

Cohn-Sherbok, D. (ed), *Interfaith Theology: A Reader*, Oxford, OneWorld, 2001

Di Martino, V., *Roman Ireland*, Cork: Collins Press, 2003

Fanning, B., *Racism and Social Change in the Republic of Ireland*, Manchester: Manchester University Press, 2002

Faughnan, P., *Refugees and Asylum Seekers in Ireland*, Dublin: UCD, 1999

Faughnan, P. & Woods M., *Lives on Hold: Seeking Asylum in Ireland*, Dublin: UCD, 2000

Fernando, A., *Sharing the Truth in Love*, Grand Rapids, Mich: DHP, 2001

Gidoomal, R. and Thomson, R., *A Way of Life*, London: Hodder, 1997

Harris, Nick., *Dublin's Little Jerusalem*, Dublin: A&A Farmer, 2002

Hogan, E. M., *The Irish Missionary Movement: A Historical Survey 1830-1980*, Dublin: Gill and MacMillan, 1990

Hurwitz, C., *From Synagogue to Church*, Cork: Pauline Publications, 1991

Hyman, L., *The Jews of Ireland: from Earliest Times to the Year 1910*, Shannon: Irish University Press, 1972

Irwin, G. & Dunn, S., *Ethnic Minorities in Northern Ireland*, Coleraine: Centre for the Study of Conflict, University of Ulster at Coleraine, 1997

Kapur, N., *The Irish Raj: Illustrated Stories about Irish in India and Indians in Ireland*, Antrim: Greystone, 1997

Kertzer, D.I., *Unholy War: The Vatican's Role in the Rise of Modern Anti-Semitism*, London: Macmillan, 2002

Keogh, D., *Jews in Twentieth Century Ireland*, Cork: Cork University Press, 1998

Keown, D., *Buddhism, A Very Short Introduction*, Oxford: OUP, 1996

Knitter, P., *Introducing Theologies of Religions*, Maryknoll, NY: Orbis, 2002

Lentin, R. & McVeigh, R. (eds), *Racism and Anti-Racism in Ireland*, Belfast: Beyond the Pale, 2002

Longley, E., *Multi Culturalism – the View from the Two Irelands*, Cork: Cork University Press, 2001

McDermott, G. R., *Can Evangelicals Learn from World Religions?*, Downers Grove, Ill: IVP, 2000

McGuire, M., *Differently Irish: A Cultural History Exploring Twenty-five Years of Vietnamese-Irish Identity*, Dublin: Woodfield Press, 2004

Netland, H., *Encountering Religious Pluralism: The Challenge to Christian Faith and Mission*, Leicester: Apollos, 2001

O'Sullivan, O., *One God, Three Faiths*, Blackrock: Columba, 2002

Price, S., *Somewhere to Hang my Hat: An Irish Jewish Journey*, Dublin: New Island, 2002

Rivlin, R., *Shalom Ireland: A Social History of Jews in Modern Ireland*, Dublin: Gill and Macmillan, 2003

Rolston, B. & Shannon, M., *Encounters: How Racism Came to Ireland*, Belfast: Beyond the Pale, 2002

Ryan, M., *Another Ireland*, Belfast: Stranmillis College, 1996

Sacks, J., *The Dignity of Difference*, London: Continuum, 2003

Siev, S., *The Celts and Hebrews*, Dublin: The Irish Jewish Museum / Shannon: Centre for International Co-Operation, 1995

Stackhouse, J. G. (ed), *No Other Gods Before Me?*, Grand Rapids, Mich: Baker, 2001

Taggart, N. W., *The Irish in World Methodism 1760-1900*, London: Epworth, 1986

Tennent, T. C., *Christianity at the Religious Roundtable*, Grand Rapids, Mich: Baker, 2002

Thompson, J. (ed) *Into All the World: A History of 150 Years of the Overseas Work of the Presbyterian Church in Ireland*, Belfast: Overseas Board of the Presbyterian Church in Ireland, 1990

Wright, C., *The Uniqueness of Jesus*, London: Monarch, 2001